THE SKY IS
NOT
THE LIMIT

Published by John Blake Publishing Ltd,
3 Bramber Court, 2 Bramber Road,
London W14 9PB, England

www.johnblakebooks.com

www.facebook.com/johnblakebooks
twitter.com/jblakebooks

This edition published in 2017

ISBN: 978 1 91147 427 2

British Library Cataloguing-in-Publication Data:

A catalogue record for this book is available from the British Library.

Printed in Great Britain by CPI Group (UK) Ltd

1 3 5 7 9 10 8 6 4 2

Designed by Crazy Monkey Creative
Ground Floor, Halls Orchard Barn
Oak Lane, Apuldram, Chichester, PO20 7FD

Edited by Michelle Golden

Papers used by John Blake Publishing are natural, recyclable products made from wood grown in sustainable forests. The manufacturing processes conform to the environmental regulations of the country of origin.

Every attempt has been made to contact the relevant copyright-holders, but some were unobtainable. We would be grateful if the appropriate people could contact us.

John Blake Publishing is an imprint of Bonnier Publishing
www.bonnierpublishing.com

THE SKY IS
NOT
THE LIMIT

AMANDA NEWTON

JOHN BLAKE

Acknowledgements

I don't think it is possible to list all the people I wish to thank individually, but those who have been with me throughout my amazing journey giving me love and support, I wish to thank from the bottom of my heart.

Contents

Prologue - The Hill 1

August 2015 5

September 2015 22

October 2015 43

November 2015 60

December 2015 76

January 2016 96

February 2016 111

March 2016 123

April 2016 135

May 2016 148

June 2016 162

July 2016 175

August 2016 190

Epilogue 200

Most people sit down at a desk to write a book.
With my disability I chose to write my book standing up
in my standing frame.

Prologue – The Hill

Nobody knows what lies around the next corner. We sail on the sea of life with a gentle breeze in our sails. Sometimes the sea becomes turbulent so we batten down the hatches and ride the storm.

Little did I know that when I awoke on the morning of 9th August 2015 I was about to embark on a journey through the biggest, wildest, scariest storm I could imagine. I was training for a half Ironman triathlon. This involved a 1.2-mile swim, a 56-mile bike ride and finally a 13-mile run. Since my four children had settled into school I had taken up running (as well as going back to study for a degree in Theology!). It wasn't to lose weight. I had been very lucky and found myself, even after having four children, the slimmest I had ever been. Embarking on a mile run one day, in order to test my fitness, although I looked pretty healthy, almost gave me a heart attack! From that moment on I was determined to improve my fitness levels and give myself the best chance possible of being healthy. I wanted to enjoy playing and running around with my grandchildren not just sit by watching them. At this moment in time I don't think I had ever been fitter.

My running had developed and improved over the years. I had started with the Bognor Regis 10k. This had led on to half marathons and finally the ultimate running challenge, the London Marathon. Unfortunately training for these events led to some injuries. As I increased my mileage I suffered with a tight IT band. This is a very common injury in runners and sometimes referred to as 'runner's knee'. Determined as always to still run a marathon, I took to the water to maintain my fitness as I couldn't run. Unfortunately I was no water baby. Oh my, what an eye-opener this proved to be. With a mix of every swimming stroke I knew and a little of my own made-up one too, I took to the local pool. On reflection I am actually quite surprised that I didn't find myself being dragged out of the water by a life guard, who may easily have thought I was drowning. I managed about 15 lengths on my first attempt. That wasn't continuous though. I had to stop nearly every length to catch my breath, and of course a quick chat. Nevertheless I did it, and again I now had the same desire to improve my swimming as I originally had when I started running. With a combination of the swimming and a little running and limping thrown in for good measure, I made it to marathon day: Brighton Marathon 2014. I had decided to run on behalf of Guide Dogs for the Blind, a charity close to my heart as I had been puppy walking for them for a couple of years now. It didn't quite go according to plan, as these things rarely ever do! I likened it to childbirth which also, in my experience, has never gone to plan and almost hurts as much. A marathon, nonetheless, and my ultimate running goal achieved. The sacrifice for this achievement was no running for almost six weeks. My IT band had tightened so badly around my knee that it had pulled it out of its socket. I needed to rethink my fitness regime. This was when I discovered triathlons. Again I started small with the Arundel Triathlon sprint distance, and worked my way up and onwards to tougher events. That year, 2015, I had signed up for my biggest challenge to date. The Hever Castle half Ironman distance. Training was going well and I had managed to follow a training scheme. That particular Sunday morning my training programme required me to cycle the full 56 miles. I had run 13 miles the day before and swum 1.2 miles on Friday. I got out of bed shaking off the morning aches and pains plus a little stiffness from yesterday's run. I was pleasantly surprised, though, as overall I felt really good.

As usual I was totally disorganised for my ride and rushed around the house trying to locate my cycling gear, helmet, shoes, water bottles, gels and causing utter chaos as I went. Things always took twice as long where I was concerned and always involved everyone helping me as I had no system or structure really to anything in my life. I just hurtled along at 100 miles an hour in everything I did. Finally I was ready to go. As I closed the front door I could have sworn I heard those within the house sigh with relief.

Once on my way, the destruction and chaos I had caused that morning was soon forgotten. It was a beautiful summer morning early in August. The breeze was warm and the sun shone down brightly. I felt I was totally in my element. I loved being out on my bike. I felt free from all my worries and problems. It was a place where I could get away from the hustle and bustle of normal life and just embrace the beauty of nature. I reflected on how lucky I was to be fit, strong and healthy and able to get out on such a glorious day. In my usual non-structured way, I had no route planned but made it up as I went along. After about forty-five minutes I found myself up at the top of Bury Hill. I really don't have a clue what led me there that day. I have only ridden down it once and it wasn't the nicest of experiences. It is a notoriously dangerous hill and ironically enough a boyfriend of many years ago had crashed his car on it. Fortunately, although he sustained a few injuries, he was out of hospital after a few days.

I took a photo of the view from the top and told myself just to take the descent easy. I had nothing to prove, I was just out to enjoy my last long ride before my half Ironman. As to what happened that day I still don't quite know. One minute I was at the top of the hill with the day planned out ahead of me. A nice bike ride, home, bath and a roast dinner with the family. Next minute I was hurtling down the hill at almost 50 miles an hour totally out of control trying with all my might to apply the brakes. They just weren't working. What on earth was I going to do?

I didn't really have time to think. I could see the last sharp left-hand bend ahead and I knew that at the speed I was travelling I would not make it. I was worried about being hit by another car and also of falling onto the road and getting road rash. I could see bushes and undergrowth on the opposite side. I felt that to head for them would be my best option. They would break my fall and give me a soft landing. Without further hesitation I pulled out and over to the other side of the road. It was really hard to control the bike as I was going so fast. Goodness knows how I avoided being hit by any oncoming traffic travelling on the hill. It was always pretty busy and cars always travelled up and down it way too fast.

I breathed a sigh of relief reaching the other side of the road. I must have had my eyes shut as I don't remember seeing anything. I remember the ride being pretty bumpy and being scratched by brambles and branches. Suddenly I felt the worst pain ever. It felt as if someone had whacked me at full force with a metal object in the base of my back. I found myself in a crumpled heap on the ground shocked and confused. My whole body was engulfed in pain, I have never felt anything like it. I could feel a warm fluid creeping up my legs. At first I thought it was blood. Then the realisation dawned on me: it wasn't blood, it was paralysis. At that point I just knew I would never walk again. I kept saying over and over in my head, 'You silly, silly girl you have really gone and done it this time.' I was in a real mess. The most frightening thing though was the fact I was struggling to breathe. I thought it was the strap on my helmet, so I managed to release it and take it off. This made no difference at all. I had a searing pain in the right-hand side of my chest. Every time I tried to breathe the pain went through me like a knife. I felt panic inside but knew this would only make matters worse. I had to stay calm. I struggled to take in air wondering as I gasped whether this breath would be my last. I tried to find my phone but it had been thrown from my pocket. No phone, completely hidden from the road by all the undergrowth, paralysed, completely broken and fighting just to breathe, I really thought I was going to die. I just wished I could be unconscious so I didn't have to lie there waiting for the inevitable to happen. I even looked around me for a rock so I could hit myself over the head and end it all rather than lie there suffering.

This was when the thought of my family came into my head. A light was suddenly switched on. I wasn't going to let myself die. My children would kill me if I didn't come home again. Vic wouldn't cope as a single father of four. I had so much to live for and I was going to fight to the bitter end. I focused all my energy and attention onto the road that I could see through the bushes above me. My only hope was that a cyclist would come by very slowly climbing the hill and I might be able to cry for help.

I waited for what seemed like an eternity and low and behold a cyclist came past. I could just see his wheels, so with all my might and in such pain, I cried out. I thought my cries had been in vain as he carried on by. I felt defeated. I would have to wait such a long time for another cyclist to appear. Suddenly a head popped over the bushes. I have never felt more elated, relieved and overjoyed in my life. 'Please help me I'm badly injured. I've broken my back. Please dial 999 for an ambulance,' I muttered. The rider seemed a little too laid back for my liking and I kept getting very impatient with him, poor man. He said I was fine and held my hand. Later when we met again when he visited me in hospital, he told me he knew I was in a really bad way, he just wanted to keep me calm and not frighten me. He also said that he wasn't holding my hand as such but keeping a check on my pulse. Finally the ambulance arrived and Gary, the name of my knight in shining armour, was replaced by paramedics. My terrible ordeal of being alone and fighting for my life was finally over, and as I was loaded into the ambulance my adventures as a spinally injured person were about to begin.

August 2015

8th August

Anyone fancy a 50-mile or so fairly hilly bike ride at about 8am, tomorrow? Being the social butterfly that I am, company is always welcome.

As I stood at the top of Bury Hill and took this picture I was thinking about how great life was. Little did I know that this would be the last time I would ever stand. I had no idea of the life-changing event that was just moments away.

9th August

No easy way to tell you all this, my back brake failed on Bury Hill this morning and I lost control and ended up in a massive bush, but typical me managed to collide with a signpost. As a result I have broken all my left ribs, broken my collarbone and broken my back. I don't want to make anyone sad or upset but I'm not going to walk again – I will now at least win all my running races in my wheelchair. Feel free to visit when I know more of what's going on and where I am, as I will be in hospital for a while and we all know I like a good chat.

After the drama of being rushed to hospital and assessed by the trauma unit had subsided, and Vic and the children had gone home, I felt I needed to inform all of my friends about my accident and the fact that I would never walk again. How do you begin to tell everyone something like this? I had just witnessed the initial anguish and upset of the news on my immediate family members. It broke my heart. I didn't want people to be sad for me. After all, I had almost died. At that moment I felt so lucky and relieved to be alive, lying safe and warm in a hospital bed. I was so grateful at being rescued from my not so comfortable bed in the undergrowth. I felt so blessed with everything I still had. Not sad at what I had lost. I felt the best way to inform everyone of my situation was on good old Facebook. I don't think I realised at the time the impact this would have on people and I certainly didn't expect it to make front-page news. I would later learn of the impact my accident had on them when they came to visit me. Many of them told me what they were doing when they saw my post and how it made them feel. I was about to discover just how loved and special I truly was!

10th August

I am really sorry I haven't managed to look at all your messages and can't even begin replying, but I am overwhelmed with your kindness and I am such a LUCKY, LUCKY LADY even with all this going on! Kitty wants everyone to know I'm fine and that I have major surgery tomorrow on my broken back, so fingers crossed it goes well. Thank you all so much again… I'm very, very blessed.

11th August

Oh my, every time I look at Facebook I am blown away by your kindness and thoughtfulness. I want to try and keep you updated, so I hope you can bear with me. I am going to theatre for a big old op in half an hour, so I'll try and let you know as soon as possible how it goes, but it might not be today; my spine is being straightened. I messed it up quite a bit, and rods and screws are being inserted to support it. I crushed a vertebra which they might remove. My spinal cord is damaged, but I have the best surgeons and doctors around and of course the best friends who are keeping me very strong and positive. Thank you so much.

Having a serious accident leaves you feeling very vulnerable in so many ways. In an instant I had gone from being a fit, strong and independent woman to being totally useless, weak and very broken. I was totally dependent on the nursing staff around me for everything. I couldn't do anything for myself, this also included going to the toilet. Everything was totally overwhelming. I just trusted implicitly what I was being told and nodded in agreement to everything. I don't actually think I had much of an idea what was going on. I put all my faith in those around me. To be honest there wasn't much else I could actually do. I'd only ever had one very minor operation, ironically enough only a couple of months before. Now I was undergoing two operations in as many days. One of which was very serious. I think the fact that I was on a high amount of morphine for the pain meant I spent a considerable amount of my time in cloud cuckoo land. The important thing for me was to get better as quickly as possible and get back home again to my family. In the meantime, I would keep everyone updated with my progress on Facebook. Everyone had been so supportive and caring, I wanted to let them know how I was getting on as everyone was so concerned. It also gave me something to focus on and it helped me remain positive. I had so much to fight for and be strong for. There was no way that I was going to let this get me down or break me.

12th August

I have had a bit of a busy day today but have Wi-Fi again. I have had a second operation on my shoulder, with metal plates and pins as I'm going to need a strong upper body to work with to help with my rehabilitation. I'm going to Stoke Mandeville (not sure of the spelling) after the weekend to begin my journey. I will be in a wheelchair, but that's cool and I'm fine with that. I am very lucky to even be able to write this message and I am still as mad as a box of frogs, and think all the staff know me very well now, too. Just keep me in your thoughts and stay positive too because although I can't reply to all these wonderful messages, I am working my way through them when I'm not being poked or prodded or rolled or examined, and they are lifting my spirits no end. At the moment I'm eating ice cream, yum yum, and have a big grin on my face!

13th August

An eventful spinal X-ray done this morning, in the midst of a flood in the hospital basement. Water coming in through the ceiling and all over the floors and doctors, nurses and staff rushing everywhere trying to stop it. A bit daunting for everyone concerned, but afterwards I spent time with my family and celebrated Meg's amazing AS results, of whom I am so proud. Then I had some lovely friends visit me throughout the afternoon. It felt like my birthday with all the cards and presents, peaches AND ice cream tonight, but the cheese in the cheese salad was a bit rubbery.

15th August

Good morning! I've got to share a dream with you that makes me chuckle. I hope it makes you smile, too. I dreamt I was at the edge of the pavement waiting to cross the road in my all-singing, all-dancing pink wheelchair. Some people on the other side started shouting out and calling me 'spethial' because of my appearance. I immediately sprung out of my wheelchair and chased them and on catching them, said, 'Do you know, I may be in a wheelchair and I can't walk, but I'm bloody clever and I got a degree in the summer!' It made me smile when I woke. Every day so far has been challenging in some way or other and obviously, according to my dream, my new life is going to take some time to come to terms with. The challenges are so trivial in comparison to the marathons and some of the races I've run. I can now sit up in bed, (whoop whoop) pour my own water, feed myself without dropping it all down me, and some other delightful challenges that I will spare you the gory details of. There are many challenges yet to come but every day I will get stronger and achieve more. Ever the optimist me, so bring on today, and whatever delights and downfalls, I will give 100% TO MAKE IT THE BEST ONE I CAN.

13:14

In case anyone is interested I've added a picture from my own personal experience, I think a good old Lidl helmet can't be beat!

16th August

I'll spare the details but today has been the toughest day to date. I've made a lovely friend, a seventy-five-year-old lady in the bed opposite. I gave her one of my teddies to cuddle as she was missing her daughter, and in return she gave me a little fan. Sorry I can't reply to any private messages, I'm too pooped today to do that, just snuggling down to sleep – sweet dreams.

To those reading the above post I'm certain many things would spring to mind when I mentioned that today had been the toughest day so far. Perhaps the pain had been at its worst or perhaps I was really missing my family. I don't think that there would be many, if any, that would actually guess what it was. A spinal injury doesn't just affect the ability of the body to move; it has a massive effect on the body as a whole. My body went into complete shock after the accident and that included my digestive system and bowels. I hadn't been to the toilet properly since two

days before my accident. I was never very regular at the best of times and the whole accident had brought everything to a complete standstill. Over the previous week I had learnt that suffering a spinal injury meant your method of emptying your bowels completely changed anyway. My spinal injury meant I could no longer empty my bowels naturally, so I would have to do it manually! At 5am every morning every lucky spinally injured patient has the delight of being woken up to have little golden suppositories shoved up your bottom. They are left for half an hour to an hour to take effect, to soften anything that may be up there. At 6am a nurse comes round wearing some gorgeous latex gloves and inserts her finger inside your rectum, rotating it to stimulate your internal sphincter. (I never knew we had two sphincters!) This in turn encourages any waste substance up inside to come out onto a special bed sheet that has been laid underneath you. Everything is then taken away and disposed of and you are given a good wipe. Now this is what causes people with a spinal injury the most trauma, upset and depression. It feels degrading and demoralising. As a fully functional able-bodied human being, fitter and healthier than most, I was reduced to not even being able to wipe my own bottom. To add insult to injury, at that time this how I thought my bowels would be emptied for the rest of my life. It was only later I was told otherwise and given the options available to carry out the task myself.

17th August

Brilliant day today. I've had some physio and have been getting myself up to sitting, that six-pack is certainly coming in handy! Oh, and tomorrow the big adventure really begins as consultants and physios are waiting for me to arrive at Stoke Mandeville at 2pm! I'm excited and optimistic and a little scared and uncertain, but I am in the best place I could be. Can't believe my silly little selfie made the national paper, too!

19:11

The day just gets better and better! Living the pampered dream of having my legs removed of hair by Lydia Powell and Anna Bagnall – I really am cherishing all my lovely friends with all their gifts, help, cards and words. At this moment I really couldn't be happier!

The move to Stoke Mandeville stirred up mixed emotions. Besides feeling excited, I felt scared and nervous as I was moving further away from my children, husband, family and friends. I was very worried how the family would keep it all together and manage without me. I was a stay-at-home mum and my children were my world. That had now come crashing in all around me. In the beginning when I was first admitted I told myself that I would be home in about six weeks. I also told myself that it wasn't that bad, as Vic and the children were only just down the road. Now all of a sudden I was being whisked off up the M25 to Stoke Mandeville. That meant the journey to come and see me would take a couple of hours. I also had a feeling that my stay was going to be longer than six weeks. No one at Brighton had actually given me a timescale. Their job was to patch me up so that I was well and strong enough to be moved to a specialist spinal hospital. Apparently I was going to the best too! Stoke Mandeville was home to the Paralympics and I had been chosen from many spinally injured patients to complete my rehabilitation there. Beds at Stoke Mandeville were in demand and consultants selected patients with a strong and positive mental attitude. I fitted this criteria. The waiting list was three months plus, but I had jumped to the front. What an honour to be going! But so far away. So many emotions all jumbled up in an emotional washing machine. Life was certainly throwing challenges at me left, right and centre, but I was going to take it all in my stride.

18th August
OMG – I'm off. Let the adventure begin!!
12:03
Just a quick message in case there's no time later due to loads of tests, scans etc. I've arrived safely and it looks amazing, I've already ordered roast beef and Yorkshire pudding for dinner.

Today was quite an overwhelming day with the move from Brighton to Stoke Mandeville. It was also a very emotional day, involving my running

club. They wanted to raise money for me to buy a pink wheelchair so they had pink Hello Kitty T-shirts printed. They sold these to any runner who wanted to take part in a 'Run for Mandy' around Chichester harbour. There were loads of pictures taken and a video too. It was very moving for me to see a vision of pink runners on Facebook just showing how much they all cared for me. One picture struck me in particular. It was the colour of the sky the night they did the run. I have never seen such a beautiful sky in my life. The deepness of the pink was breathtaking. It made me feel like someone up there was telling me everything would be alright. A sign of good things to come. Pink sky at night, Mandy's delight.

19th August

Lovely day today and a beautiful bunch of flowers as well. I can feel I'm getting stronger. As my legs won't work, I find I am gesticulating with my hands and arms more. This nearly proved a disaster as on the way down for another X-ray I was waving them about excitedly talking to the porters and nearly managed to send a big picture of sunflowers crashing to the floor as I hit it with my excited arm!

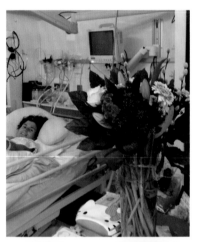

20th August

Busy day today. First hair wash since the accident and boy did it feel sooo gooood! I had a ride in my hoist to my wheelchair as my back is still healing, but soon I will be leaping in it from my bed. I visited the gym and coffee shop in my chair, which exhausted me completely. Another beautiful display of flowers were delivered, too. I realised today just how long my road to recovery is, but little steps and I will get there! Thank you all for your visits, messages and presents, you're really keeping me going.

The day couldn't have started any better with my first shower in almost two weeks. I will never forget the experience of lying on a plastic bed a bit like a large paddling pool with the hot water cascading over my skin singing 'I'm Singing in the Rain' at the top of my voice. Once back on my bed I insisted on being left wrapped up in soft warm towels with the sun streaming through the window. I didn't want to face being rolled backwards and forwards and side to side in order to dress me. All the movement used to make me feel nauseous. I didn't want to ruin the moment. I promptly fell asleep for two hours! I remember my children also doing that as newborn babies after having had their baths. It was exhausting. I was also really beginning to realise just how long the road to recovery was. I managed a mere twenty minutes in my wheelchair later that afternoon after recovering from my first shower. I felt so sick and dizzy, I thought I was going to pass out. The pain was unbearable as well. I guess even with the morphine I was on, that breaking the amount of bones I had, the pain was going to be pretty intense.

I felt useless. I had to be hoisted into my chair. I couldn't even manage that on my own. Although I was obviously stronger than I had been a few weeks ago I was still so weak. I thought back to how I used to think nothing of running 13, or cycling 50 or 60 odd miles and still get on with my day-to-day activities. Now here I was and I couldn't even get out of bed on my own. I could have very easily felt completely defeated but I just kept focusing on all the lovely experiences I was having. That was my survival mechanism. The flowers were beautiful, the cards and the presents. It felt like every day was my birthday and still I felt so special. I took each day as it came. I could not look into the future, as a sense of panic would rise up inside me and for every negative that I would experience, I was determined to find a positive.

21st August

I've had a perfect afternoon with some of my favourite people today, but I have a little confession to make! At the moment my wheelchair and I have a bit of a love/hate relationship going on. I am in an HDU (high dependency unit) and can only progress to rehab when I can stay in my chair for four hours. This is where the problem begins. I have broken all my ribs on my left-hand side, front and back. I have to be strapped tightly into a very rigid brace to support my broken back. My ribs become quite squashed and when I am lifted into my chair I have to sit in a really straight upright position. The pain is nothing like I have ever experienced in my life. My blood pressure dropped to 89/46, which is quite low I believe, and I kept nearly passing out! Yesterday I managed twenty-four minutes and today I managed almost fifty, but I have to go through it all again tomorrow! I had thought it would be a little easier than this, but boy, oh boy how wrong was I.

22nd August

Today is going to be a great day! I am so pleased as I have just received an email from the cyclist who stopped when he heard my cries for help in the brambles. God only knows what would have happened if he hadn't stopped, but I will be eternally grateful that he did.

13:31

I don't want to overload people with Facebook posts but today really is turning out to be great, some people's kindness is simply just overwhelming. These balloons have just been delivered by Worthing Excelsior Cycling Club, a club I've never even heard of before, and they've never heard of me, yet they took the time and effort to think of me!

20:16

Another favourite person, my little brother (Joe senior).

20:20

This may sound silly but today truly has been a GREAT DAY. It was decided by the doctors that my ribs are so swollen from yesterday's wheelchair experience that I could have a rest day today. So many visitors, so many presents, so much laughter, so much fun. I never knew a hospital bed could be such a lovely place to be. But when surrounded by those you love, it doesn't matter where you are, and that is very true!

Gary Gathergood is the name of the man who found me on that fated day just a few weeks earlier. I think the name is very ironic as Gary came along and 'gathered me good'. Obviously I had thought a lot about him whilst in hospital as I am pretty sure that if he hadn't come by, then I wouldn't be writing this book. It's very hard to put into words the feelings you have for someone who has saved your life and to comprehend exactly what that means. It's something that no one ever really considers having to deal with. I have just come to realise, probably more than many, since lying in the bushes, just how precious life really is. I am forever grateful that Gary got in touch. It was going to be the beginning of a very special and unique friendship.

23rd August

Wakey-wakey, rise and shine. All showered and dressed and waiting to see what delights lie ahead of me today.

14:55

One WHOLE HOUR accomplished. It materialised that the staff yesterday strapped me in my harness incorrectly and crushed my ribs rather than support them! Today's experience was 100 times better and I feel like I've run a marathon now. I'm exhausted but happy!

I decided to treat my rehab at Stoke Mandeville like a training programme for a marathon. It was certainly proving to be as tough as one. In order to progress to the official rehabilitation ward downstairs, you are required to sit in your wheelchair for four hours. Anyone in the running world will know that a four-hour marathon is a really respectable and sought-after time. Psychologically for me this was the best approach to adopt. It would mean I would be able to tolerate the pain better as marathon training definitely brought with it its fair share of aches and pains. It would also help me with the good days and bad days. Running brought with it good and bad runs. Ones where you felt you were flying and you covered miles with ease and the runs where you felt you were struggling through thick treacle and every step hurt. You knew if you had a bad run you would have a good one again, so if I had a bad day in my chair I knew a good one would follow. I also understood how important the rest days were. This helped me listen to my body whilst building my time up in my chair and not beating myself up if some days I needed to take it easy and rest.

24th August

I love this picture of my Rosie dog and her two new friends! I saw my consultant today and he said that I am healing well but I have eleven broken bones that I need to be gentle on, three in my back, my seven ribs and my collarbone. He says I should take it easy and not expect too much in my chair at this stage, but just rest and heal. I can manage that I'm sure. Oh, and I gave an interview today with a man who sells stories to all the girly magazines so I may get a story in one of those as well! He is phoning me back tomorrow, I'm quite excited about that!

20:33

The kids have been trying to teach me to use Snapchat – I think it's called. This picture has just popped up of this young man, all kitted out in new uniform ready for his new adventure to begin! My children are the really brave ones carrying on with life whilst I lie here getting better, when really I should be looking after them. I am proud beyond words of them all.

25th August

I certainly know how to start my day. I'm lying in bed watching *Postman Pat Special Delivery Service* and now *The Clangers* – I LOVE THE CLANGERS! The day is going to get better, more lovely visitors are coming including Vikki the second guide dog I trained and her owner. I haven't seen her in four years!

14:37

Some things in life are just so incredible. It doesn't seem possible they can be true! Martin visited me today with Vikki, which in itself was such a delight, but it then turned out he is friends with Matt who has Unity the German Shepherd I trained and have never heard from. We had a three-way conversation round my bed with Matt on the phone about the dogs and how amazing they are, whilst little Vikki slept curled up in my hospital curtain. I kept rubbing my eyes as I thought I was dreaming the whole thing up. Ever since I had my accident things just keep getting better and better. I can't believe how lucky I am!

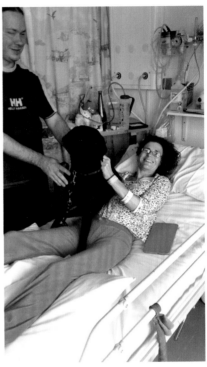

26th August

I can finally breathe a sigh of relief and put a post up. I've been waiting all day for an X-ray of me in my horrible back brace to see if it has been fitted correctly, but after all the fuss it has been postponed until tomorrow! I am a bit of a wimp where my brace is concerned as it isn't the most comfortable of things, but I have to wear it for three months, so I've just got to get on with it! Good news is I no longer need to be put in a harness to get into my chair, my upper body strength, even with the breaks is paying off. Finally, I had a moving moment on the hospital roof with another wheelchair patient today. There is a lovely veranda up there where we can wheel our chairs. I met a man there who really made my heart go out to him as he was just sobbing. I asked him if he was OK and he told me his life was over. He was never going to walk again! I told him that his life was just beginning, but different! We were both alive and both out in the sunshine. I said it was OK to cry, but he was still a very lucky man and that I'd try and come and find him tomorrow. He smiled and I told him he had a nice smile and I hoped to see it next time we met! I really keep thinking about him, I hope he becomes happier and comes to terms with what has happened to him.

I was always treated very well at Stoke Mandeville. A bed became available by the window in HDU and one of the nurses moved me straight into it. Theoretically we weren't allowed flowers, but my window sill when I moved beds looked like the front window in a florists. I also had more 'clutter' than anyone else in the ward, which was also seen as a health and fire risk but the lovely housekeeper just managed to squeeze it all into my little cupboard by my bed.

It was so lovely too when Martin brought Vikki to see me, she even managed to have a sneaky cuddle on my bed. I'd always perceived hospitals as being quite stuffy and regimented – I guess in a spinal hospital where people undergo real life-changing tragic injuries, rules are bent a little to bring patients some happiness and comfort when they are dealing with their losses. During my time at Stoke I experienced some of the happiest times of my life.

I learnt during my time in hospital that people discovering that they weren't going to ever walk again usually take a little time to adjust. Other people were certainly not always as positive as me. I met many patients with spinal injuries and heard their stories of how they came to be at Stoke. I did my best to help them see the positive side of their situation, although at times it was hard. Not all people were as accepting. One friend actually refused to eat or drink for three months and had to be fed intravenously. Being a nurse on a spinal ward was certainly a hard job dealing with people who really were not coping well with their new life. I just thanked God daily for my sunny disposition.

27th August

I'm not brave all the time, I had a wobble today! I have to have blood tests several times a week and my veins have become rather shy and it flipping hurts. Today when I had to have the test done I felt myself well up and nearly cry. I've been told it's the little things that can trigger off the tears rather than the big things, but I'm happy again now as I have lots of lovely visitors coming in later, and the postman has been and I have lots of cards and a present too!

19:21

A very important post for me – I HAVE JUST HAD THE HAPPIEST HOUR IN MY CHAIR. I have endured the time in my chair to date but today with the help of some lovely friends I really enjoyed myself. The pain seemed less and the time flew by instead of me clock watching. Such a milestone as I will be spending many hours to come in a chair and now I'm looking forward to getting in it tomorrow instead of feeling apprehensive! I have really turned a corner today and feel very accomplished.

20:49

Oh and yes, I met my friend on the veranda again and he did indeed have a lovely smile for me today and no tears!

Blood tests still make my toes curl, so to speak. Funny how I could endure all those injuries and yet wimp out over a simple blood test. I think it was the manner in which they were done. Quite often you would be woken at about 7am to be told you needed to have blood taken. Mornings could be tough anyway, let alone with a blood test being chucked in for good measure. I got crafty though and realised you couldn't have them done if you didn't have your identity bracelet on. I lost mine accidentally on purpose. This resulted in a visit from my consultant querying my refusal for a test, a new bracelet being issued and a blood test taken five minutes later!

28th August

Another 'Happy Hospital' day. The man who found me in the bushes at the side of the road is coming to visit me! I'm not sure of a date yet but I'm so excited. I'm not quite sure what to say to him, it's going to be such a strange and wonderful experience I'm sure. I can't wait!

20:22

My dad and I don't always see eye to eye and we have been having a few little 'issues' with me walking again. He is adamant that I will! Tonight he said something that moved me to tears as the issue reared its head again. He just said, 'Mandy you don't understand, even if you don't walk again in this world when I die I will wait for you at the gates of heaven and then when your time is nigh and you come and join me you will walk towards me and join me, you will walk towards me and I will hold you in my arms!'

29th August

Yippee! The wheelchair relationship is growing stronger. I managed my longest time EVER today 1 hour 40 minutes. That's the equivalent to a nice easy 10-mile run so I'm up in double figures, which I'm so happy about, and almost halfway there in time for my wheelchair marathon challenge of four hours. Lovely time spent with more great friends and the day made completely perfect with my four beautiful brave children. Feeling blessed.

30th August

A strange man just turned up at my bed today. I said, 'I'm sorry but I don't know you – I can't see you very well I haven't got my glasses on.' He said 'I put them in the saddle bag on your bike three Sundays ago at the roadside!'

The night Gary visited was a very difficult experience to actually describe and put down in words. We just talked to each other about how the meeting on 9th August had felt for each of us. Compared to our first

meeting tonight was very normal and relaxed. Gary was a very quiet, calm man. This explained his manner at the roadside. He had also worked in the emergency services as a coastguard. He held my hand, not to comfort me, but to keep track of my pulse. He also kept talking to me, not to be annoying as I had thought at the time, but to keep me conscious. He also knew that I was badly injured but told me that I wasn't because he didn't want to frighten me. He informed me that as a coastguard he had seen people with less injuries than me who had not survived. That thought sent shivers down my spine. I knew that fate had brought us together that day especially as Gary never usually rode the route he rode that Sunday. He only travelled that way because his friend had ridden that way earlier in the morning, and it was a challenge for Gary to therefore ride that way too and try and beat his friend's time. That day, 9th August threw two totally different people together in such an unlikely situation but as a result would create a very unique friendship, a friendship I would never have with anyone else.

31st August

Happy Bank Holiday! I don't like to post too much in one day but I managed two hours and a very important ten minutes yesterday in my chair! Over halfway now. I lay awake last night thinking a great deal about Gary, the man who rescued me! I really do owe him my life. I was in quite a bad way when he found me, worse than I remember! I really am very, very lucky. As a result, I think today I am going to have a chill-out day and rest and just put my feet up and relax.

16:23

So much for putting my feet up. I'm not very good at staying still and relaxing so I was delighted that two of my running friends were happy to accompany me on my first BIG ADVENTURE, to Asda!

I have always been spontaneous so I guess it was no surprise that I decided to make my first trip to Asda without having planned it first. I remember the experience very well. Pushing the whole way there was very tiring and I was so determined to do it myself. I did need a little help up a few slopes which now I would fly up without a seconds thought. What I remember most was the moment where I found myself in an aisle completely alone as my friends were somewhere else and feeling so vulnerable and small. It was a feeling that took me by complete surprise but didn't last long as my friends eventually came to the rescue. Everyday I was achieving a little more and everyday I was getting a little bit stronger and that is all I could hope for.

September 2015

1st September

Lying here looking out of the window to another day with MORE visitors thinking how lucky I am to have so many friends! Fareham and Mandy Sayce are visiting later, which I think will induce a few tears as I will officially be saying goodbye to my little girl as she goes off to finish her training elsewhere. I ache this morning but it is a good ache like you get after a long run. It shows I'm getting stronger, and I'm so looking forward to being able to get down to that gym. Hope all my friends have a good day, too.

Seeing Fareham made me realise just how important assistance dogs are to people with disabilities. A few weeks ago I was able-bodied, training this dog to be a companion and pair of eyes for a blind person. How

things can change so drastically, as I was now a person with a disability who would benefit so much from such an amazing dog. It was only now with my new life in a wheelchair that I was able to fully appreciate how truly beneficial these pups are to people who are less able than others.

2nd September

About to embark on my first session in the gym. I am given a drug that helps raise my blood pressure slightly as mine is quite low. Apparently one of its main ingredients is found in speed! Mandy in a gym in a wheelchair on speed, goodness knows what will happen!!

16:56

Best day ever today! Spent half an hour in the gym and got on an exercise machine that someone with my injuries isn't really allowed to. Sssssshhhh, don't tell the doctor. The physio and I talked about training for Rio 2016 Paralympics. She told me 'the world is my oyster' and if I want it I should go out there and grab it! Also did two and a half hours in my chair which included eating lunch with the lovely Keith Hardwell to keep me company.

The first day for me in the gym and such a feeling of mixed emotions. The last time I did a gym workout I was so fit and strong. I had my legs, my strong, toned active legs. Now they were incapable of doing anything. My legs were strapped to pedals on a cycling machine and a little motor worked my legs round. I met Sarah my physiotherapist at Stoke for the first time. She was lovely and so positive. There was hypothetical talk of Rio Paralympics, but in hindsight I realise it was just words of encouragement to help me work harder. There was no way in my broken state I was ever going to make Paralympic standard in just a few months but it was lovely to dream and talk about it.

3rd September

Awake thinking about my brave, strong young man starting his first day at secondary school today. I've just spoken to him and said how proud I am and how he will be in my thoughts all day! Thinking of all mums

and children going off to school to begin a new adventure today, too.
19:14
A pretty long post I'm afraid! Today has been a bit of a roller-coaster of a day. With mixed feelings concerning Joe, I went to the gym and couldn't even sit up on a bed holding a table – I nearly fainted. I got sent straight back up to my ward to go back to rest even though I was due an X-ray and was really sick just as I was about to be moved to my bed! Feeling better for this I insisted I went for my X-ray, which was a right palava, too. The X-ray guy asked if I was going to stand for him to take it, which made me really laugh, but I think he was mortified, poor man. I don't think he could believe how I brushed his comment off by laughing either, as he said my good sense of humour and smile were infectious! After the X-ray I passed the gym and was asked if I wanted to come back and finish my session, so I thought 'go for it girl' and had a really great time. All in all I managed three and a half hours in my chair – sometimes maybe days that don't start all that great turn out to be pretty damn good and to round it off nicely, Joe had the best day at school ever!

Sometimes life in hospital was tough. So much to deal with both physically and mentally. Some days were just such a battle to keep going but somehow I managed to find the strength to carry on and push myself further. That young boy had to start his first day at a new school while he carried the worry of his mum in hospital recovering from a serious accident. He knew that although she was still his mum, things were never going to be the same again. If he could cope with all he was dealing with, the least I could do was get myself fit and strong so I could come home and be there for him and my other children.

4th September
Had an update today on my injuries – silly girl that I am I did a flipping good job of breaking my back. I have two rods and eight bolts holding it together but it is still pretty unstable! As a result I have to wear my sexy black brace every time I get in my chair to hold everything together so I don't break any more for three whole blooming months! This is a bit of a pain, literally, but in the grand scheme of things it's a little burden to put up with. I had lovely friends here at the time when I was told the news and that is what makes things easier. I really am so fortunate. I have

been inundated with cards, presents, messages, visits, phone calls, people raising money, the list of the support and love and care I have been shown is phenomenal! I'm not anything special, I'm just Mad Mandy, but I have been made to feel so special and loved that with so many beautiful people in my life spurring me on I can achieve anything!

21:20

A little post before bed. I am pretty bed bound and can't sit up more than 30 per cent, so my bed is my space for nearly all of my activities and they are all done lying down – therefore there are lots of spillages and accidents! During the time I've been here you will be amazed at the things the nurses find when they change the sheets. We've found satsuma pips, raisins, and even wrapping paper stuck to my bum! Numerous little pill pots, sweety papers in abundance, crisp packets, Hello Kitty stickers, a pen, a phone charger, a flip flow valve (google what that is), and tonight I filled the bed with breadcrumbs which had got everywhere including a lot of places they shouldn't! It has become a standing joke as to what delights will we find in Amanda's bed today, but it certainly makes us giggle!

> *I think on the whole my black brace got me down more than anything else. It made me feel very conspicuous. I was trying to come to terms with a whole new identity for myself sitting down permanently. This in itself is hard enough. On top of that I had to wear my black piece of armour, as that's what it felt like. It was so restricting and caused significant discomfort and pain. I also felt it made me look ugly. Any pretty top I wore was just covered by it, and black is my least favourite colour. I had to tell myself the good that it was doing me. It was helping me mend and that it would not be for ever.*

5th September

Had a bit of disappointing news. Apparently my story isn't 'Christmassy' enough to make it to the women's magazines, so the writer and I are planning to try and make it more seasonal. We are contemplating dressing me up as a fairy and hoisting me up to the top of a fir tree outside the hospital and taking a photo!

21:13

MISSION ACCOMPLISHED – four hours and fifteen minutes wheeling round and round the hospital in my chair. When have I ever been known to sit still! Rehab here I come!!

Over four hours in my chair! What a major achievement. I had such a psychological battle with my beloved chair. I used to dread getting into it because it hurt so much. I wanted and needed to feel comfortable, happy and confident in my chair, not miserable. My chair was now my legs and my means of being mobile. It was my way of life. My legs were, in my opinion, my greatest assets. I was really happy with my legs and I wanted to feel the same about my chair, but it was proving to be a lot tougher than I thought. It was impossible to stay in one place whilst in it. The pain in my back would become unbearable if I did, so I just had to keep wheeling round and round. Even if I was having coffee with someone I would have to keep wheeling around the table we were sat at. The pain was easing a little now though, and I was having less morphine to control it. I was really making progress.

6th September

OMG! Whilst I've been laying here mending broken bones, my amazing daughter has learnt to do some amazing flips and somersaults, and she doesn't even go to gymnastics! This is the reason why I have to get strong and well because I have four of the most beautiful, brave, gorgeous children at home who need their mummy back – I really need to get my arse in gear.

20:29

There are many things I'd like to share on here regarding my new life as a 'T10 Complete Paraplegic' and a member of 'ASIA' (ASIA stands for American Spinal Injury Association). I'm being technical here, but I feel it might make people uncomfortable. Close friends who have visited now understand the more gritty stuff, but for a couple of days I have thought about sharing something and I think I will. It's funny lying in bed not being able to feel your body from just below the waist. My legs feel very heavy like I have a great weight on them. Over the past couple of days my legs have taken on a new life of their own, especially the right leg! My toes move all on their own and I have no control and no feeling in them and a couple of times they've kicked, again quite a weird experience and apparently it can be quite upsetting. They feel like they have their own identity. For this reason I've been referring to them as 'hims'. I ask the nurses if they could 'cover him up for me' or 'move him for me' and yesterday I decided to do a Mad Mandy thing and name them. My left leg is Bert and my right leg is Ernie. Apparently this has never been done before but it just makes the nurses laugh and quite a few are calling them that already! It makes me laugh, too. My brother and sister-in-law are even going to buy me some Bert and Ernie socks. One lovely nurse has actually given them personalities! Bert is the good, quiet one and Ernie is the naughty one! I guess what I'm trying to say is that it's just important to keep a sense of humour and laugh about stuff however bad it may actually be and I have laughed so, so much since I've been here and really just tried to turn any negative into a positive.

Whilst looking through Facebook I came across a video a friend had posted of a child doing a round-off back flip to a backward somersault. This is quite a difficult sequence to perform for a young gymnast. When I looked closely I could not believe that it was actually my youngest daughter Amelia, who didn't even have lessons. I actually had to watch the video a fair few times just to make sure it was her and take in what she was actually doing. I worried on a daily basis about my children and how they were coping with what had happened to me. They were continually proving to me that they were dealing with things even though I knew it must be so hard for them. They never ceased to amaze me and make me proud.

Today also marked the day where I came up with the idea of naming my legs Bert and Ernie. Even now the names have stuck. There was almost the temptation to name the book Bert and Ernie too, but it was felt it might cause problems with copyright! Bert is still the better behaved one and Ernie always causes trouble. If ever a shoe falls off it is always Ernie's. Giving them an identity has certainly helped me cope better with the fact they spasm and do things of their own free will.

7th September

Spinal patients on the whole suffer with lower blood pressure than you able-bodied folk! The legs are no longer able to pump the blood up round the body as quick, so it's very easy to get light-headed and giddy, plus lying down for long periods of time gives you head-rush too. I also suffer from sickness which can happen, and my pain relief also makes me sick. I got to the gym this morning, and this will make you laugh, all I am learning to do at the moment is sit up on my own. I never realised how hard that could be! When you have no feeling in your legs you don't have the ability to balance, so your brain has to train your core muscles to help you balance again in a totally different way. I tried so hard and looked like a flipping weeble. I was sweating, I had to manage 30 seconds in an hour just sitting at a table with my hands in front of me. I got to 24 seconds in 20 minutes, and because I was trying so hard and the brace was so hot I came over really sick and almost passed out again. I've never been known to take things slowly. I was rushed back to my room but luckily I managed to persuade the nurses to just let me get some fresh air. I then got more pain relief, just paracetamol and anti-sickness drugs, and went back down to the gym and completed the weight session on my timetable too. It is unbelievable how much of a challenge these things are but all spinal patients go through it. I'm just unlucky as I have more broken bones than most and I am hindered massively by my harness, but this is only temporary and every day I am getting stronger. I'm in bed now eating jelly and ice cream.

18:14

Drinking Hello Kitty champagne to celebrate a new life, new adventures and amazing friends and family.

20:23

Oh I know I've shared lots already today, but you can imagine how delighted I am that a lovely nurse has literally just come round and told me that she has found out that Stoke Mandeville have their very own Triathlon Club – things just keep getting better and better!

8th September

They tried to make me go to rehab and unlike Amy Winehouse I said OH YES, OH YES, OOOOH YEEEEEEESSSSS… and here I am! The journey to recovery really begins.

9th September

Today it's exactly a month since this new adventure began on Bury Hill! I find that quite hard to believe as I have experienced and learnt so much in such a relatively short time. I do have wobbly moments, I wouldn't be human if I didn't! I just try and learn all I can from them and move forwards towards becoming stronger and more determined. I still have a very long way to go though, so every day I just take little steps and take on every new experience and challenge with a smile and don't look too far ahead. Oh! I discovered on my first night in rehab that some spinal patients can really snore!

A whole month on from the date of my accident. It is quite hard looking back to take in all that has happened and how fast I had progressed. As I have said in my Facebook posts it hasn't all been plain sailing and I have had wobbly moments. I also mentioned in an earlier post about there being nitty gritty bits that didn't feel appropriate to share on Facebook. Now though I feel that I can. As I mentioned earlier, since my accident my toilet routine has been all over the place. In the beginning I suffered with really bad constipation. This can be quite common in a person with a spinal injury. Sitting down all the time means that the digestive system can become a bit sluggish. Most people with a spinal injury take laxatives on a daily basis to keep things moving. This can spell disaster if the amount of laxatives taken isn't correct.It can also take a while to get the balance right. The bowels are a very hard part of the body to establish a routine with. This can mean lots of very embarrassing accidents, which was what I was discovering. My bowels were behaving very badly. When they were stimulated at the 6am 'stir-up' time nothing would happen but they would like to surprise me by waking up just as I got in my chair and went down to the gym. There would be an ominous smell and I would have a little feel on the seat of my chair and 'hey presto' a nice surprise would be waiting there for me. These little surprises caused me the biggest wobbles and the same can be said for many people suffering from paralysis as well. Not walking is the easy thing to deal with. Sorting out a reliable regular toilet routine is probably the hardest thing to achieve. The nurses were very good about them.I would go back to bed and get help to clean up. When my curtains were drawn I'd explain that I was having a 'Poo Party'. I tried to make light of the situation but it really did get me down. I think it would anyone.

10th September

Really feeling on top of the world today – I have been a busy bee! I had an hour of physio, a meeting with my case manager, a meeting with my rehab advisor, a trip to see my old friend Poppa on the way to Asda, AND a grand total of five hours in my new buddy – my chair… we have really bonded at last!

11th September

Good morning – some very early Friday morning spinal injury facts:

1. Only 0.06 per cent of the British population have a spinal injury and 75 per cent are male – see, that's how special I am!

2. Spinal injured people don't sweat from the point of their injury down, so no more sweaty, cheesy feet for me!

3. There is a blood transfusion called a 'Safe Cell' transfusion in which you are given your very own blood, and I've had one.

4. There is a type of pain commonly experienced by spinal injured people called neuropathic pain in which the brain goes into overdrive, trying to send electric messages to your legs. As a result it makes your body buzz and fizz all over like you are completely covered in stinging nettles. I've experienced it a couple of times and ironically enough when it happens all I want to do is get out of bed and run it off!

5. Other senses become extremely heightened as a result of the injury. My sense of smell is really acute and I can feel goosebumps on my legs when I'm cold and other weird sensations.

6. Many patients also experience muscle spasms and quite often these are a way of your body letting you know that something is wrong below your injury level, as you no longer have a sense of feeling.

7. And finally, to date, the nurses have found in my bed: a teaspoon, a banana, a bracelet and a packet of chewing gum.

12th September

Only just woken up. I was too excited to sleep last night! Sixteen years ago a baby boy entered my world. This afternoon he will enter my hospital room and make me the happiest lady alive as I will be sharing his sixteenth birthday celebrations with him. Happy Birthday Jacob Worne!

22:11

All tucked up in bed after a really special day with my birthday boy and the family. Quite eventful too as we almost set off all the hospital alarms with the candles on the cake! Very, very hard to watch them all leave me tonight and walk away, as all I wanted to do was walk away with them. I did cry (I do share the tears with you all too) and it did me good! It left me feeling more determined than ever to just keep working as hard as I can to get home to be with them all again as soon as possible.

I was so lucky that Jacob's sixteenth birthday fell on a Saturday, so even though I was in hospital I wouldn't miss out on seeing him. My brother Joe and I went to Asda in the morning and bought balloons and birthday cake. I remember so well coming back and attempting to blow up balloons but not having enough air in my lungs to be able to. The spinal injury had affected my tummy muscles and it was very hard to cough, sneeze or laugh so trying to exhale long breaths was also difficult. As I had also punctured my lung and broken so many ribs this also played a part in my lung capacity. I had to do breathing exercises to encourage my lung to work properly again and to also avoid it becoming infected. Fluid could build up in the bottom of my lung where I wasn't using it properly and could cause infection. This did actually happen at Brighton and I was on intravenous antibiotics before I moved to Stoke. I had actually developed hospital induced pneumonia. Celebrating Jacob's birthday with him was so special. All my children seemed to have grown up overnight since my accident. I guess they had to. Saying goodbye, as I mentioned, almost broke my heart. No parent ever imagines being parted from their children and unless you go through it you can't actually imagine what it is like.

13th September

Yawn, yawn, stretch, stretch. It's amazing what a few birthday celebrations can do to a girl! I've been pretty pooped today but I still managed to get out of bed for a bit. I'm trying to be brave and come off some of the heavy pain relief drugs but I'm a wimp really and it's quite hard. It means I've had to have extra chocolates to help – well, that's my excuse anyway!

14th September

Been dozing in bed on and off this morning – after all no one likes getting up on a Monday – and I've just found a 'good morning' message from the man who found me in my bramble bushes! It's funny how he is someone I have never met before that day, and he was only with me for such a short period of time – but he has had such an impact on me since! I got such a feeling of happiness reading his message, I suppose in a way I relive the feeling I had when he popped over the embankment and found me. I'm really chuffed he has stayed in touch and likes to know how I'm getting on.

19:19

A day full of laughs and meeting new people. In my physio lesson I had to try and balance and put marbles into plastic cups without holding on! It's something we all take for granted that we can do, until your legs become paralysed. It required every ounce of concentration I had, but I kept laughing because I kept losing my marbles and a man on another bed kept making me giggle! I also met a patient who has done seven Ironman events and due to a cycling accident is paralysed from his chest down! We talked for ages and he said his biggest challenge now is just to be able to use his fingers again. Patients in here bond well because they can relate to each others experiences. He got his dinner and couldn't cut it up, but I was able to help him and he was grateful that I did it!

15th September

I think by now everyone can see that I am using Facebook as a window to my heart. All my emotions, both happy and sad, I share with you! Today I can tell you that I am just a little bit worried, it's something that I've never even contemplated worrying over in my life before, but it is now such a critical part of it. The dreaded pressure sores that render so many wheelchair users bed-bound! I have a red mark on my heel that if I am not really careful, could develop into a nasty sore; the blood supply is cut off from areas of the body if we lie in one position for too long. When we have feeling, we move because we become uncomfortable. I don't have feeling and I can't move on my own yet anyway! Luckily my heel has been spotted quite early and we are keeping all pressure off of it. Checking my skin's condition will become a really vital part of my daily routine and I will have a long-handled mirror to check my back, and areas I can't see! On a funnier note though, I've just had a shower and the nurse found a 'Passed British Safety Standard' sticker stuck to my backside!!

21:28

Settling down to sleep and I have been lying all evening on my side with my bottom facing the open ward door, where all the visitors, doctors and nurses and patients pass by. It's warm on the ward so I have been lying without a sheet over me, as I assumed the nurses had put my pyjama shorts on. I have just felt down and realised I am butt naked. What a lovely treat everyone must have had, as they walked by!

The thought of pressure sores used to frighten me so much, but I think the staff at Stoke Mandeville deliberately scare you and make you paranoid about them so you don't get them. I know a lady who was in a 'sand bed' with an ulcerated pressure sore. She was in Stoke when I arrived and I left before her. I have also heard stories of people who deliberately get pressure sores so that they have to stay in hospital. I know one man who has been in Stoke Mandeville for three years because he cannot cope with the real world any more. He has become completely institutionalised. So many things I never knew about and so many new things I am learning.

16th September

Oh my goodness, I haven't laughed SO much in my life! If I didn't have a catheter in I really think I'd have wet myself! Jo Brennan and I have just relived some old school days where she tricked a supply teacher into believing her name was Alice Springs, except today she pretended she was Amanda Worne. I put my name down for tea in the canteen, but unbeknown to me, I have to wheel myself down there to get it. No one else can get it for me, not even staff. I am limited to hours in my chair because of my sores, and now I'm in bed, so the dinner is thrown in the bin and I go hungry. We hatched a little plan – Jo got in my chair, put a blanket over her legs and wheeled herself to the canteen, and told them she was me! Imagine my absolute delight and the sheer laughter between us when she turned up ten minutes later with my dinner on her lap. Something I will laugh about for many years to come, and one to tell the grandchildren!

17th September

Some of you may find this interesting, it's not meant to be upsetting as I understand what is happening. Debs Pacey is giving me some beauty treatment and my legs can react to the pain but I don't feel it. The nerves in my body and legs feel the pain, but the messages produced don't travel up to the brain to tell me that it's hurting. It doesn't give any indication that I will walk again, my body just likes to tease me. Oh, and apparently I have really bad hobbit feet!

22:16

I have learnt probably the most important thing since my accident tonight: never to have my legs waxed again! Autonomic Dysreflexia or AD is a symptom experienced by the body when it feels pain and it doesn't know what it is. If the pain is not detected it can be life-threatening! My body had a mild AD reaction to the pain from the waxing, I had fuzzy vision, drowsiness, temperature and a bad headache! Often it is due to a bladder problem or some other symptom. I feel OK now and phoned Debs Pacey and had a good laugh about it, as neither of us knew I would react this way, and she was doing me a favour out of the kindness of her heart – again, another important learning experience! We decided next time she visits she will bring a razor and shaving foam.

18th September

I feel very fortunate that I have been here now for almost six weeks and I still have friends who are prepared to travel such a long way to see me, when invariably the journey takes longer than the time we have together!

A visit from lovely friends today bringing more presents, but most importantly, bringing me lots of happy laughs, and helping me maintain my good spirits. It's also nice when they are able to chivvy the nurses along to get my drugs that I need to get up in my chair.

> Whilst in hospital it's not only physical change you have to learn to deal with, it's also the effect the accident has on you mentally. The mental impact of never being able to walk again is harder than the physical, in my opinion. It has a knock-on effect on so many things. One thing it has a big effect on is friendships. People who care about you react in different ways towards your new situation. In hospital you are warned that a lot of people who regularly visit you whilst you are there will stop visiting you when you get home. This is when you discover who your real friends are. I am a very sensitive person at heart and this is something I have found quite hard to deal with. People managed to travel 100 odd miles to see me in Stoke Mandeville, yet now I'm home and only 10 minutes down the road, I never see them at all. Some people I have lost touch with completely. I try not to take this personally. I understand that things have to go back to normal. Peoples lives are busy. For me though, my life will never be the 'normal' I had for so many years. I can no longer do all the things I used to do so easily. Some things I still need help with. This is a time when I need my friends the most. I have experienced many emotions dealing with this fact; hurt, upset, bitterness even rejection. I have had to learn that this is the normal part of the process and just to accept people for who they are. The people who really matter are the ones who are still here with me now and give me support and they are the ones I am truly grateful for. I have also learnt autonomic dsyreflexia is usually experienced by people of a higher injury level, but I still feel poorly if something hurts or is wrong with my body below my injury level.

19th September
(feeling determined)

Yesterday I finally managed to visit the Paralympic stadium where it all began, with two very fit athletes, and I did a lap of the track! Today I felt really poorly and when I got up I was really sick, but it was such a

beautiful day I was adamant I was going outside! I visited the track and was going to do two laps but my brother convinced me to do three. I'm hoping to try and get up to a 10k before I leave.

20th September

I'm spending my last night in St. George's tonight. My consultant moved me down to rehab as soon as a bed became available, as he wanted me to make progress. Rehab is divided into George and David – my consultant's ward is David but he put me in George until a bed became available on his ward. I have Joseph as my final destination. I keep just finding my feet and getting settled and then I get uprooted again! As always, I am trying to be positive, but I have to be honest and admit I don't want to move, as it means new routines and explaining all my medical needs to new nurses, and getting to know all the new patients on the ward. Four moves in six weeks is a fair few moves I'd say!

On top of everything else, changing wards can also be quite unsettling. You become used to the people in the ward around you and build up relationships. The nurses also become familiar with your needs, both medical and physical. You are encouraged in a spinal hospital to be assertive and tell the staff what your needs are. You must become very bodily aware and independent, knowing yourself if things aren't as they should be. Moving from ward to ward means you have to start building up friendships with patients and rapport with nurses all over again. It becomes quite draining. Little did I know that at this stage I still had quite a few moves to come.

21st September
(Monday morning Mandeville fact file!)

Firstly, I hope I haven't already mentioned this, but one of the side effects of some of my medication is that it makes me really forgetful. Secondly, this is a little lavatorial, so, if you'd rather, don't read on.

Spinal injuries affect your gastric movement, this includes your ability to pass wind. Gas builds up and gets trapped very easily, and the elasticity of the stomach is reduced after a spinal injury, so quite often my tummy is as tight as a drum! I have no ability to control my farts! They don't happen very often, thank God, but when they do and if I'm in a situation where they aren't quite appropriate, I can't feel them coming. I don't have the ability to clench my bum cheeks and hold them in! Prime example, a lovely twenty-one-year-old lad, training to be a doctor, helping me put my shoes and socks on, and suddenly an ominous smell hits my nostrils, you can't deny it, so I'm having to get used to saying, 'Oops, sorry, pardon me!' Thing is, if any of you visit me, you can always let rip and blame it on me, coz I'd be none the wiser anyway!!

19:50

I've arrived at St. David's. I already know two patients here and one is a really amazingly, positive strong lady and a real pleasure to know. Unfortunately, there are a few whinge bags who seem to do nothing but moan! It's fair to say there is a big staff shortage on the spinal unit, and I have been late to physio on many occasions. I've even had my physio come up and literally drag me out of bed as she has been so frustrated, and it is a bit disheartening I admit, missing my valuable physio time. Listening to the other two women whingeing continually about the food, the staff, their wheelchairs, being uncomfortable, their pain and their tea being cold, makes me feel a little sad for them, as it actually won't make a difference and it won't make them feel better! I am made up at this moment as it is hot and stuffy in this hospital and for the first time EVER I have a fan by my bed! I have it on full whack and I'm lying here in bliss, but I have to make sure I have nightwear on this time and I'm not exposing any naughty naked body parts.

After being in hospital for a time, especially as a spinal patient, you start to forget the worry or embarrassment of people seeing you naked. You have fingers inserted up your bottom every morning, bed baths every day or showers which are always accompanied by a nurse – nudity becomes the norm. A spinal unit, well Stoke anyway, holds a 'no knicker' policy in bed. This is to help alleviate bed sores caused by undetected creases in underwear. For this reason when nurses come and help you in the morning you have a 'modesty', which was a pillowcase, to cover up your private parts. I unfortunately used to get a bit lapse with my modesty. Some nurses were like little angels. We would talk for ages and ages when they came in the morning to give me a bed bath or shower and neither one of us would even realise I was naked. We shared lots of personal details and stories. Quite a few had sad stories themselves to tell, which

I think was what led them to work where they did. I remember an older, quite stern nurse walking in whilst I was chatting to one particularly lovely nurse and we both got a telling off for my modesty being missing. 'Amanda, where on earth is your modesty?' she cried. Apparently it wasn't only for my benefit but some nurses themselves felt uncomfortable staring at so many naked patients on their rounds. I guess I had never viewed it from that perspective before.

22nd September

Oh how HAPPY am I! Having a fantastic first day on good old Dave's. Was meant to have routine blood tests but they were cancelled (oh shame) and I was washed and dressed and all ready for the day before 9am! Even the whinge bags had a good old laugh with us last night, too!

23rd September

I am having to introduce some new words into my vocabulary – carefully, slowly, methodical and vigilant. These are very unnatural words for me. Yesterday I had a narrow escape from quite a nasty injury, I had plucked my eyebrows and two and a half hours later found the tweezers in my back! Very, very luckily there was not a mark where they had been. I've also bruised my feet by using them to open a door. This is such a learning curve for me and it actually may do me some good but it's a little tricky for one who is used to doing things at 100 miles an hour!

21:33

Feeling very pleased with myself earlier after a successful solo shopping trip to Asda to buy ingedients to make flapjacks in the morning, I made my way back to the hospital. A very helpful shop assistant had tied my shopping to a handle of my wheelchair. I crossed at the zebra crossing and prepared myself for the steep incline on the other side. Halfway up the weight of the bag took its toll and I started rolling backwards. All of a sudden out of nowhere three people rushed to my rescue. I managed to save myself just before they got to me. I think we all had a bit of a fright, but we ended up having a right old laugh after. I think I'm going to be a bit of a Frank Spencer of the wheelchair world!

24th September

Well I tempted fate by saying I was making flapjacks. I'm such a little sparrow (well, that's what the nurses call me). I have ended up with a red patch on my sacrum (at the base of my very little bottom) and I'm on bed rest as the chair will make it worse, BUT I was allowed to go to physio and I am SO glad I was because I STOOD UP IN A STANDING FRAME!! For the first time since the accident six weeks ago I was in the position I've been so used to for forty-four years and it was just the best feeling ever – the whole gym knew I was standing, I was so elated! My physio expected me to pass out after one minute as I get so sick and giddy but I managed fifteen! There was no way I was going to let that stop me today – I'm now on bed rest but I still have the biggest smile ever on my face!

Standing since my accident was a very strange sensation. The last time I stood I had the use of my legs. I used to take it for granted. After all, it was what my legs were there for, yet now I was so grateful to be upright again. The experience was very different. I had a support in front of my knees as they would buckle without it, and a support behind my bottom. Something that used to feel so natural, now somehow felt very artificial. Although I was elated I was also sad. I knew that although I was standing it would not help me walk again. My legs in a way were dead, they felt like they were detached from my upper body. They felt like blocks of wood holding my upper body up. Ever Miss Positive though, I focused on the fact that I was my proper height again and completely vertical not horizontal like I was a few weeks before. I was again improving in strength and making progress.

25th September
I asked to stand in the frame again today, but it was for a shorter time than yesterday. I felt a bit sick, maybe pizza and Belgian bun for breakfast didn't help! I was sick as soon as I got out but felt much better and went to the track and met a load of runners and chatted to them as they went round. We all knew I liked a good chat when I ran and before I knew it I did four laps today – such a beautiful day, too!

26th September

A day of being totally spoilt with a lovely hair-brushing session complete with Argan oil, not one but two lovely foot massages and to top it all a beautiful new pair of glasses. A visit from three of my children full of smiles and laughter and full of mischief – (my wheelchair took a battering as they took it out for a spin) topped the day off nicely. I really am very lucky.

Being in so much pain a lot of the time meant that little pleasures were precious. I loved having my hair brushed or dried. Just the sensation on my scalp used to cover me in goosebumps. I loved having my feet rubbed, too. Although I couldn't directly feel it I still felt sensations deep within my body that informed me the feeling was pleasurable. Sensations and physical feeling had changed where my spinal cord had been damaged. My body worked in different ways now to tell me what was a nice sensation and what was bad. Other areas of my body had acute sensation because of the loss of it in my legs. For several weeks my back felt like it was on fire when it was touched. Nerves had been damaged and were reacting. Luckily, as they started to settle down a lot of the burning sensations dissappeared. This was such an adjustment for my body to make, massive in fact, and it was going to take a year or so until things really settled down for me completely or as much as they were going to.

27th September

I don't mind admitting I actually feel a little sad today. In fifteen minutes I should be starting the swim on my biggest Triathlon challenge ever – a half Ironman distance. It's the reason why I'm lying in this bed! I trained so, so hard until the day I crashed. Six days a week in fact, and although I was really, really nervous I felt excited because I'd never been that fit in my life. Little did I know I would be faced with an even bigger challenge on the Sunday I set out for my 50-mile ride! The positive thing is – because we all know I look for the positive – I have developed a good mindset from all the training and determination and I know there are good days and bad days but you just keep plodding on because you get there in the end and the rewards are so worth it!

I realise now that I wasn't actually training for my Triathlon but for the amazing adventure that I was now on. Ironically enough, I hadn't been training for my Triathlon, this wouldn't have happened, but it was the fitness from my training that was helping me recover so well and was even responsible for keeping me alive when I lay in the bushes. Someone who wasn't so fit might easily have died from the shock of all the injuries as they lay waiting to be found. Gary told me that he had been a coast guard and that he had seen people with injuries less serious than mine who had not survived. Although I had missed out on my Triathlon I was lucky to be alive. Life was actually proving to be very good, with many beautiful, lovely things happening to me. I really was starting to think that I was meant for this.

28th September

Firstly, a beautiful picture of Fareham looking very grown up and secondly I've had a really, really productive day today. Things are starting to come together! I did an amazing transfer from my chair to a plinth, which is a type of bed, ALL ON MY OWN and sat very controlled for over a minute. I had a 'goal-planning meeting', which speaks for itself, and one of my goals over the next three weeks was to take my own shoes and socks off. Well I came back to the ward and did it straight away! Sounds so simple and we do it without thinking, but a massive achievement for me and I held each of my feet lovingly like you would an old friend.

20:33

Ever since I had my accident this song has come into my head so many times. Today lots of you have sent me things to keep me positive and to keep my spirits high, so I thought I'd share my happy song, too! I've had a really lovely day again with fab friends and my beautiful daughter and her handsome young man, Thomas, and a picnic in the sunshine.

The song was 'Three Little Birds' (Don't worry about a thing) by Bob Marley.

21:39

The highlight of an action-packed evening on David's ward is all of us female patients squealing at the daddy-long-legs that have got into the ward throughout the evening. I kill myself with laughter, as I am in bed unable to move or escape as the flipping things flap around above me. I have to rely on my more able-bodied friends in their wheelchairs to rescue me and chase them away with rolled-up towels. I just pull the covers high over my head and make loads of silly noises!

29th September

I hope people aren't getting tired of me saying I've had an amazing day, but yet again today has been BRILLIANT! I beat my seven x Ironman friend in a rowing race on the rowing machines so now we have a competition on our hands. Then I went to Asda and was really naughty and shook the bottom shelf to make the cake on the top shelf fall off! I did a session on a leg bike and finished off with some weights to build up my arms. It isn't alot but I am now lifting 3k weights with each arm rather than 2.5k! I had visitors ALL day as well, and two lovely ladies had a workout of their own giving Bert and Ernie a haircut. To top it all I spent six and a half hours in my chair – I don't know if you can tell, but I'm BUZZING!

30th September

Good sunny morning. I have woken up and my arms are killing me, the gym has taken its toll. I am now debating whether I will have to move around like a little worm wriggling on its tummy!

17:01

When I was a child and having a bit of a grump my dad always used to say, 'Mandy, what's the first thing you do in the morning? You get out of bed, well some people can't even do that!' Well guess what? This morning for the first time since the accident I did just that, I got out of bed and into a chair all on my own being supervised by a physio. The feeling of liberation and independence was overwhelming, I really felt today for the first time that I am getting my life back again! I was still in my pyjamas and the physio wanted me to get back into bed again but I just couldn't bear to do that, so I went off to physio in my jimmy-jams with a spring in my wheels and the biggest smile ever!

October 2015

1st October

I'm shattered, I've been to the seating clinic and tested out loads of new cushions that will look after and protect my tiny little posterior. Then I went and stood in my frame for a bit. I went on the gym handbike and rode 3km in just over half an hour, which is a marked improvement on my last attempt. I had wheelchair skills to follow and learnt to do 'pop wheelies' and had some lovely visitors to round the day off! Over seven hours in my chair and I'm scared that when I fall asleep I will be so tired I'll sleep right through until Saturday!

Now I'm home I miss the gym being just down the corridor. I also miss the timetable and structured days; it made motivating myself that bit easier. Everything was more accessible and required very little effort to get to. I seem so out of the habit these days of training and it is proving very hard to get myself back into a routine again. On the flipside though, I realise now how obsessed I was with being fit. I didn't see as much of my family as I do now. I love the time I have free without every second being filled with either a swim, a cycle or a run. I find time to just sit and ponder and watch the world go by. I am here for my children even if I'm not doing something specifically with them, I am just about. Time is so very precious and something that once it is gone we can't get back. I will get fit again but there is no rush and when I do I will get the balance right. Never again will it take over my life like it did before. I realise now that life is too short to let that happen.

2nd October

Lying on my bed feeling a little nervous, but also excited as I have my first hydro lesson today. I have also learnt another interesting fact. I won't know if I'm out of my depth because I can no longer feel the bottom since my injury. And will my legs sink or float?

19:38

I've had another fab day but I can't stop thinking about how many people are, and have been, working really hard and are raising money for me this weekend. I find it really hard to comprehend, that it's me the money is being raised for! I have loved raising funds for guide dogs in the past, but it feels really weird having money now being raised for me. I really feel I should be helping or getting involved too. Thank you, thank you THANK YOU – I really am lost for what to say, but I'm just a very, very VERY LUCKY LADY with lots of friends with enormous hearts!

> *Hydro lessons, swimming or water activity of any kind make any spinal patients nervous for one main reason in particular. The biggest worry is having a bowel accident in the pool. With a spinal injury, because you can no longer feel or control your bowels entering water is a risky business for you and anyone else who happens to be in the water. At hydro you are always asked before you enter the water if you have been to the toilet. If you are in any way unsure that your bowels are safe you are not allowed to go in. Since leaving Stoke I still have hydro sessions and having an accident still worries me more than anything. I certainly avoid an Indian takeaway the night before as that could spell complete disaster! Despite the worry, being in the water is the best feeling ever.*

3rd October

Having a lazy morning just chilling in bed. I think I am really starting to master this wheelchair thing – I did nine hours yesterday! Physios are reluctant to take off my anti-tip wheels, though for the life of me I can't think why. Bert and Ernie took to the water like a couple of ducks in hydro. They floated like they were inflatables and completely with a mind of their own. Apparently a lot of spinal-injured patients' legs sink like lead, I guess I got lucky. I finally made my flapjacks too, and rather than burn the kitchen down, it took over half an hour to fathom out how to turn the blasted cooker on!

I don't mention in my post but today is my mum's birthday. I won't elaborate too much but I have always struggled with my relationship with my mum. Having my accident has brought us closer together. It has really made me realise that although I don't always feel that my mum loves me, she truly does. It must be heartbreaking to see your child at any age go through what I have. I know she is very proud of how I have coped and I know that she loves me no matter what. Many good things come out of something bad and it is important to focus on that.

4th October

Feeling excited this morning. I'm starting to really take control of my body management in preparation for coming home for a weekend in the near future. Last night I injected myself with an anti-blood-clotting injection for the first time. I'm not a great fan of needles, like a lot of people, but at least I could inject somewhere I couldn't feel. I'm also starting to do some of the more nitty gritty things myself! They may not be the most pleasant but they give me independence, which is so important to me. I'm more than happy to share the more unpleasant things if people want to know more. I won't share openly though, as some people might not want the information, so please feel free to PM if you want all the gory details.

I've shared some nitty-gritty information with you already concerning the bowels but I haven't talked about the bladder. My spinal injury means that although I can feel when I need to have a wee I am unable to send the messages to my bladder to make it open. It is therefore necessary to use a catheter. Depending on the patient a catheter can be used in various ways. I am lucky and can now self-catheterise. This means when I go to the toilet I insert a little tiny tube into my urethra and the wee leaves my body through the tube into the toilet. People with a higher injury level who have limited hand use often have a super pubic catheter. A tube goes in through the stomach wall and into the bladder. The tube is connected to a bag on the outside. The wee runs through the tube into the bag. The bag is emptied or changed when the bag becomes full. Another form of catheterisation is an indwelling catheter. This involves a tube up the urethra into the bladder. The tube remains there permanently but gets changed every six weeks. A bag is attached like the super pubic. This is how I started out after my spinal injury, but now I was taking some control back over my body. The bag on the tube can be detached. A valve can be closed at the top of the catheter to stop the flow of wee. When the patient needs to empty their bladder they can go to the toilet or use a plastic bottle and open the valve letting the wee out. This is called flip flow. To start, the valve is opened every hour. The bladder needs time to build up its strength again. With an indwelling catheter the bladder never fills up but remains flaccid. Now it needs to start to fill again and learn how to stretch and hold water. The time is built up between opening the valve to a maximum of four hours. Depending on the patient this is where the choice of super pubic or self-catheterisation can be made. On the odd occasion some people choose to keep an indwelling catheter. Unfortunately, using a catheter brings with it an increase in urinary tract infections and it is very important to drink lots to keep everything flushing through. I used to get very upset in the early days. I thought I would have to have a bag for wee strapped to my leg for the rest of my life. I thought I would never be able to wear shorts or skirts in the summer as there was no way I would want my wee bag, or 'golden handbag', on display for the whole world to see. It was such a relief seeing the methods available that would give me some all-important independence back and my dignity.

5th October

I've had such a laugh today with a really lovely nurse. More or less since I got up I've had a burning sensation around my tummy. I couldn't tell whether it was internal or external, as the accident has really affected my senses, so I drank a glass of vanilla milk in case it was acid indigestion – to no avail. Then I wondered whether it might be neuropathic pain just burning my skin, so I tried to ignore it. After lunch it was really driving me mad and getting itchy too, and being in the brace was aggravating it further! Finally, enough was enough and I had to get back to bed to investigate. My top was almost off before my nurse had a chance to draw the curtains, and there the mystery revealed itself: flipping brown toast crumbs from breakfast, three of which I found in my tummy button. We had such a laugh and then I nearly poked her eye out when I took my elastic multi-coloured bead necklace off, and it pinged out of my hands! To most people breakfast in bed is a treat – I'm quite looking forward to sitting at a table again!

6th October

The physio gym is sometimes the most magical wonderful place to be witnessing some amazing achievements. Today I watched Paul my Ironman friend give everything he had on the rowing machine – he is a tetraplegic with only the use of his biceps. He was feeling pretty rough and I could see it in every move he made, and the grimace on his face said it all. He was desperate to beat his last time on the machine and the physio and I were willing him on every step of the way. He beat it by three seconds and I nearly burst into tears! Jeremy, another friend whose injury is incomplete, stood today and lifted first his left and then his right foot off the ground. I could see the beads of sweat on his forehead. Everyone here is on a journey and it's a tough one at the best of times, but I am so, so lucky to be a part of it. It has taught me so much and made me a much better person. I have met amazing people who help encourage and drive me on every step of the way. My latest and toughest challenge is trying to lift myself from the floor up into my chair and it's the most difficult lift of all especially in my brace. It won't happen overnight but I really have to learn how to do it as I am bound to fall out of my chair at some point, so I will grimace like Paul and sweat like Jeremy and think of them and I know I will do it!

7th October

It all happens at Stoke Mandeville. It took me ages to get to sleep only to be woken half an hour ago to the smell of smoke and awful choking fumes. I was a little concerned to say the least and I went to turn the emergency buzzer on. At the same time a load of nurses rushed over to the bed opposite. It turned out that my friend Pauline's phone had exploded UNDER HER PILLOW – it had melted her mattress and burnt the pillow and sheet! Thank goodness she wasn't hurt. I am still recovering from the whole incident but Pauline is always as cool as a cucumber and has wheeled herself off to make a cup of tea – a large stiff drink might be slightly better I think!! I usually charge

my phone under my pillow too, so maybe a little warning to me, and anyone else not to do it in future.

The night of 6th October really brought home to me how vulnerable being in a wheelchair can be. When I awoke to the smell of smoke I felt quite concerned. Where was it coming from and was something on fire? The fumes soon became quite toxic and it was hard to breathe but what could I do. Wheelchairs were not left at the bedside at night but taken and stored somewhere. I had no way of escaping. This was when I decided to press the emergency button. In a situation like this the realisation of how helpless I was became extremely clear. I couldn't just throw the bed covers back, jump out of bed and run. I felt so scared. Thank goodness it was all over in seconds as the nurses came in and the cause of the smoke detected immediately. It isn't the greatest feeling in the world, though, feeling so weak and helpless especially as only a couple of months earlier I was so strong and capable. That is why when you suddenly suffer from a life-changing disability it is crucial to strive to do as much as you can to get that feeling of strength back again, and I vowed to myself that this is what I would do.

8th October

Such a beautiful autumn sunny day. It's a perfect day in my mind for a run and if I could I so would, but I can't. Can I just say to anyone who is, I hope you have a really, really good one, and enjoy every minute of it.

15:19

I do miss my running but there's so many new things I have now discovered that are just as much fun. I can still get my heart rate up and those endorphins flowing with a good fitness session in the gym, which is even more fun if shared with a friend! Tummy muscles had a good workout with lots of laughs too.

I don't and never have felt any resentment towards not being able to run and for those who can still run. I now just encourage my friends who do run to try and enjoy it more. I tell them not to put loads of pressure upon themselves, which quite often takes away the enjoyment. I remember doing that and it is a waste of energy. Life is fleeting, so we should try and enjoy every moment that we possibly can.

9th October

I got to have a shower sitting upright! I have to have them lying as a rule in a waterproof bed, but I had a waterproof brace on today. The water trickled off my head and down my back. It was the best feeling ever and I was so long the nurse thought I'd fallen down the plughole! Then I got to sit outside with friends and eat fish and chips out of the paper with my fingers – so many of my new spinal-injured friends can't do that because their arms and hands don't work. I kept sniffing the paper because it smelled so good! Happy, happy times.

10th October

I was very, very lucky and won a little prize yesterday! The best part of it was to donate £200 to a charity of my choice – I chose the Stoke Mandeville spinal unit. They are going to put it towards – of all things – shower chairs! After my shower experience yesterday this delighted me immensely and I can't wait until I am able to donate more money for other special spinal-unit equipment.

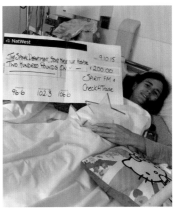

11th October

Sunday is the day I think I find the hardest. Lots of patients go home to be with family and it's very quiet here and the gym is shut as well. Being the social butterfly I am, I get bored, so today I have been helping the nurses by making beds! It's also the day I miss my family the most, having seen them yesterday. I miss having laughs and chatter with them all sitting around the dinner table enjoying a delicious homemade roast. Hopefully in a little while I will be able to go home for visits too – I can't wait!

Sundays were tough days in hospital. People posting Sunday-morning runs and posts of family outings or activities. The hospital goes into shut-

down mode, too, and I get quite lonely. I would allow myself a few tears as it is good to let things out sometimes but I would not allow myself to wallow or dwell on negative things. As well as helping nurses I would help patients less fortunate than myself. I would help the ones that had lost the use of their hands to feed themselves. This would soon help me stop worrying about my own misfortunes, as theirs were significantly greater. I would soon remember how lucky I actually was and focus on the positives again not the negatives.

12th October

I'm lying in my bed all snuggled up under crisp clean white sheets! Today I had a meeting with my consultant and he gave me the news I have been apprehensively awaiting for weeks! He gave me the all-clear to go home in two weeks' time to attend my graduation! I will still get to throw my hat in the air after all that has happened. I don't think there are words to describe how elated I am. Apparently I get a special gown to wear, which is wheelchair size!

Although I was absolutely elated to be given permission to go home to graduate it actually filled me with complete panic too. I was still really quite poorly and by no means confident with all that I now had to deal with as a person with a spinal injury. Sitting in the car for two hours worried me silly as I thought about the possibility of a pressure sore. What happened if I pooed myself when I went up for my certificate as my bowels were still not completely reliable and they never would be? What about the shoes that I was going to wear? They might dig in as my feet often swell up as the day progresses because of the change in my circulation. I might fall out of my chair. I might not be able to get on the stage at the graduation, and so it continued. I had studied for six long years for this day. I had worked harder than I had worked for anything in my life. My accident had taken many things away from me but it was definitely not going to take this from me as well.

13th October

Here is another one of my quirky spinal-injury facts! Socks are a very important thing for spinal patients and can actually cause significant damage. In many instances they have to be worn inside out. This is because the seam across the toes can dig into the foot without a person feeling it and cause a sore. Luckily for me my Bert and Ernie socks don't have a seam and are made of really soft material!

14th October

At the Stoke Mandeville spinal unit, tea is served between 5 and 6pm, during this time no patient is allowed to ring or ask for anything as all members of staff are just feeding tetra patients, those who can't feed themselves. After 6pm though, all hell breaks loose as it's a mad rush to get to the nurses first to be put back to bed! It's so funny as patients in wheelchairs all sit by their beds with their buzzers on and we all try and outdo each other to race to be put to bed first (as each of us feels that we have been up the longest or we are in the most pain). A wheelchair friend of mine told me she discovered that the best way to get put into bed was to fall out of your chair! I'm too much of a coward to do that but find chocolate bribes often do the trick!

15th October

Today it could have been Christmas Day, just minus crackers and Christmas pud! Firstly, I had hydro, where most spinal people and I experience the feeling of how we felt pre-accident, and then of course followed by the best 'upright' shower EVER! Then I managed a great milestone in the standing frame. I've been stuck at fifteen minutes for weeks feeling really sick and giddy and having to get down. Today I stood for HALF AN HOUR! I had coffee with Jeremy and Rhino Rodger, who gained his name through being tossed in the air by a rhino, which consequently resulted in his injury!! It was such a crack! Finally,
for the first time EVER, I managed to sit and balance on my bed moving my legs with ease with my hands without continuously toppling over like a weeble!

Funny how challenges and goals in my life have changed so drastically in the blink of an eye. I went from riding a 50-odd-mile bike ride to just sitting on a bench trying to shuffle my way along to the end of it without falling over. It was mentally very tough. I couldn't get my head around the fact of how useless I had become physically. I was still the same Mandy riding that bike, physically so strong, but in a split second it had all gone, gone for ever. I needed to focus all my energy on claiming back everything I could, and today just managing to get to the end of the bench was a massive achievement.

16th October

Not only do we get competitive at Stoke Mandeville about going to bed first, we also get competitive about what wheelchair we have! We are allowed to try different types of chairs so we get an idea of the type of chair we want when we leave. Today I was given the opportunity to try the *crème de la crème* of chairs on offer – the one most desired by all, a 'Quickie Helium' (funny how now I have this amazing interest for fast chairs when it used to be road bikes). Well I was so excited I zoomed out of the gym and along the corridor but was greatly disappointed – this super-quick chair was super-slow. I finally got to the ward quite frustrated, cross and puffed out. I started to curse the chair to my fellow patients only to discover at that point that I'd forgotten to take the left brake off! I guess I should count myself lucky that at least this time it worked!

17th October

I received a letter today. I was absolutely ecstatic to pass my degree, can you imagine how thrilled I am to read this! The decision to present me with the award was made back in May. I have been assured that awards like this aren't given to people because they fall off their bike!

18th October

I've had another fantastic day! I vowed to myself to have a pyjama day today as I never did that when I was able-bodied and felt that I would 'milk it' being in a wheelchair. I enjoyed a lovely bed picnic with two beautiful friends. I got out of bed 'independently' without a nurse even present to go and see them off and decided that once I was up, to pay the Olympic track a visit! Several people have been running or cycling to raise money for my racing chair, which helped motivate me on my laps, and for the first time since my accident I recorded my effort on my Strava app. I must have looked a sight though in the rain in a pair of racoon-print pyjamas and a pair of trainers, but at least I had the pyjama day I'd promised myself!

19th October

I said early on in my posts that Facebook is a window to my heart. Life weaves a weird and wonderful tapestry and this afternoon I have been confronted with my biggest, most emotionally painful challenge. Diesel, our oldest cat passed away in the arms of the person he loved the most, Megan, a few hours ago. He didn't suffer and his death couldn't have been more perfect for him. I have sobbed and sobbed and sobbed for about two hours and for a considerable time down the phone with Meg. A mother should be with her child at a time like this, so I am finding it heart-wrenching not being able to console her and her siblings. I am fortunate enough to have a close bond with my children and know that tough times will be overcome and we will be even stronger and closer. Rest in Peace Diesel, and Meg I am so proud of you for your strength.

In hospital it was extremely hard being away from my children. In the grand scheme of things the time I spent in there was very short but at the actual time it felt like for ever. I felt so helpless and that my role as a mum was slipping away from me. This was accentuated by the fact that Meggie had now had to go through the trauma of Diesel dying at home without me. Vic was doing everything and doing it very, very well. I was in hospital feeling useless. When I had a rational moment rather than an emotional one I knew that I was still as important to my children as I always had been. I was so relieved that I had been a stay-at-home mum as I had always been there for my babies. I think it had stood them in good stead for this. I knew that they were secure and happy with their father and I knew that they were strong enough to cope with everything they were having to deal with. I was more proud of them than I could ever say.

20th October

I've been waiting ALL day for this beautiful young lady to arrive so I can give her the biggest hug I have been saving for her.

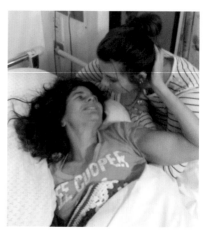

21st October

Good morning. I have just been enlightened with another spinal injury fact: I have been offered a flu jab. Spinal-injured patients are more likely to develop chest infections as the injury sustained can quite often affect the ability to cough and blow your nose! I have to say I had a chest infection in Brighton and I couldn't cough properly at all – my attempts were pathetic although I guess a whole side of broken ribs didn't help! I find it all so interesting and can't believe there is still so much to learn! Being in a wheelchair is so much more than not being able to walk. Actually that's just the tip of the iceberg!

22nd October

A really good day today. Yesterday, car transfers into the passenger side, today it was the driver's side! I was really excited as it will be so liberating to be able to drive again with hand controls, but the first thing I said was, 'Ooooh I can't reach the pedals!'

23rd October

Just been to hydro, I LOVE HYDRO! In the water you have to get right up close and personal with your physio. I had a beautiful young girl today and she had to do hip stretches with me. This means she has to stand between my legs while I'm on my back with a float to keep my head up. Today it hurt a bit as my hips were a little tight and out of practice. I rubbed my thigh to try and alleviate some pain. She is a real sweetheart and we always have a good laugh. She started giving me a few funny looks but I just smiled and carried on talking and rubbing, and then she said, 'Amanda can I ask you why you are rubbing my thigh?' I just squealed and burst out laughing as the whole time I had thought I was rubbing my own! We really had such a laugh about it, though, for the rest of the session. There is always something to laugh about here!

20:39

Such a fab day today, first a trip to the pub then a visit from Lauren the GBR tennis champ who is AMAZING in her chair, with the same injury level as me – she inspired me so much and to top it all I fell out of my chair but I'm fine and it had to be done sooner or later. Such a busy, busy day. Shooting this morning and I didn't hit anyone and then a trip to Aylsbury on the bus, lunch and then shopping for something to wear for my graduation! I'm shattered but really loved it. I cried when I got into the shopping mall! Such an amazing feeling to be back in the real world again.

24th October

Just a little insight into a shopping experience in a wheelchair. Firstly, things seem a lot bigger and cars especially are scarier when you are nearer to the ground. Your hands get mucky because your wheels pick up all sorts of dirt as you push along. People stare a bit so I give them a massive beaming smile and they normally smile back, which is good. I got caught up in the clothes on the hangers as I tried to push in between the rails, and the aisles are like mazes as I can't see over the top any more. I got a bit of an achy neck having to look up at people to talk unless I wanted to stare at their crotch, which seemed a bit rude! In the toilet I couldn't see in the mirror to put on my lipstick – big catastrophe and the hand dryer is now a hair dryer for me! I also find myself racing babies in buggies! I was lucky and was allowed to get on the bus first on the way home so jumped right to the front of the queue. It felt very surreal. I used to stand in queues sometimes at the airport check-in and watch wheelchair users go to the front and now here am I as one of those people myself.

20:47

Just been sent a picture of a beautiful pumpkin – Meg carved it for me! I really can't believe as I lie here that tomorrow I will actually be home with them all, although I'm having to stay the night in a hotel as I can't get upstairs at home yet! It's better than Christmas Eve but I am quite scared! I'm a long way away from my little hospital bubble of almost three months!

25th October

Home, sweet home!

Oh my gosh! Coming home for the first time in just over two months. You never expect that when you get up in the morning and leave the house that you are not going to return again that evening. We take our leaving and returning home for granted, just part of our daily routine. Until the day it doesn't happen, that is! To be home was just the best feeling on earth. My Rosie dog was so pleased to see me. She had been a bit poorly while I had been staying in hospital with a bit of a cough but the vet was quite sure it was nothing sinister. To see her in the flesh with her big doggy smile and waggy tail just made my heart jump for joy. I spent the majority of the afternoon with her snuggled up on the sofa. At this precise moment I don't think her or I could be happier.

26th October

A very, VERY long busy day but it couldn't have more perfect in any shape or form! Tucked up safely back in bed at Stoke Mandeville and couldn't be happier! I AM A GRADUATE!!

Wow, what a whirlwind of a day! Everything just seemed so surreal. Being in a wheelchair and graduating. Both experiences – something I really never envisaged I'd be doing. I had to go up on the stage without my shoes on as my feet had swollen up, but I didn't really care. I was so nervous anyway about wheeling out in front of all those people in my wheelchair, being shoeless was the least of my worries. BUT I DID IT and the round of applause was breathtaking and I had to fight back tears of emotion. One of the most memorable days of my life and one that when I reflect on I always find myself smiling a massive smile.

27th October

Well today was the day the brace nearly broke me! I had such a beautiful couple of days back home but twelve hours wearing it yesterday took its toll today! I didn't help myself, silly girl that I am, and was still determined to go to the gym and do a rowing time trial with two girls from the GBR rowing team. I shouldn't complain when I am surrounded by people a lot worse off than me, but I will be so pleased when the blasted thing comes off exactly two weeks tomorrow, and yes I am counting down the days!

28th October

Please, please say some prayers for my Rosie dog. I'm trying to be brave; she has been poorly for a little while but has deteriorated and has just gone off to have some X-rays. I just hope amongst hopes she is OK.

19:47

I've had an update on Rosie, the X-rays show a mass of fluid around her heart and lungs. This is either pneumonia or a tumour, so I'm waiting on more tests that will be carried out. The head nurse said she is going to try and see if I can go home again to see Rosie, but I still don't have anywhere to stay when I get there – I'm going to snuggle down and get a good night's sleep and think about it all in the morning.

So hard to believe that only two days ago I had been sitting on the sofa with Rosie and she seemed full of beans. Now she was so poorly at the vets. At first the vet thought she might have been depressed having seen me and then my departure again, but X-rays showed something more worrying. I was really genuinely concerned. Having lost my old boy cat

Diesel just the week before I could hardly take in the fact that Rosie was so poorly now, too. She couldn't die though, could she? Surely no one could be unlucky enough to be in hospital learning how to rebuild their life and lose two of their most beloved pets at the same time, could they? Sleep was definitely the best answer.

29th October

I had a lovely day with some beautiful friends who really helped lift my spirits. I even got a wheelchair with flashy wheels that made me smile, but we had to let go of our sweet, sweet Rosie a few hours ago and let her drift into a beautiful sleep. She had inoperable cancer. Oh, how I bless the fact she waited for me to come home to say goodbye. That precious time on the sofa will stay with me always. Love you my Rosie dog, sweet dreams xxx

11:59

Scrolling through hundreds of unread emails and I found a picture of my graduation. A truly happy day with beautiful memories! I'm holding on to my happy thoughts today.

I felt that someone up there must really hate me or have it in for me. I had to make the decision to have Rosie put to sleep. I couldn't be there for her and I couldn't even say goodbye. I just felt wretched. I could handle not being able to walk again but the death of my Rosie dog hit me harder than that post at 50 miles an hour. In hospital on my own with no loved ones near to console me, what could I do? Just get on with it Mandy because that's what you always do. Just hold your head up, smile and keep on keeping on. My broken bones were mending but my heart had just smashed into hundreds of tiny pieces. Life was cruel today.

30th October

A few weeks ago I was one of the less able-bodied patients on my ward and my fellow patients did a lot of things for me. I used them as my legs!

Now I am actually the only one patient on my ward with hands that work. My hands have therefore been working overtime! I have been writing letters, opening bottles and food packets, washing up special less able-bodied cutlery, feeding people, sticking name labels on food containers for the fridge, carrying trays in the canteen and even putting batteries in hearing aids! It's nice to be able to help and feel useful again, but I have jokingly said, as my hands are so precious to all of us, I'm soon going to charge for their services. I'd make a small fortune! It's actually a lot easier losing the use of your legs than your hands and I thank God every night that I still have mine.

31st October

Such a glorious afternoon in such unusually warm sunshine for almost November! My little brother visits me every weekend and treats me like a princess. Today he treated me to my first pub lunch in months and it was delicious. I also met a beautiful, very lively young black labrador called Poppy who really didn't want her photo taken! I love being outside so, so much and must admit I dragged my wheels a bit on the way back to the hospital. I know deep down though that I have a way to go before I'm ready to come home for good. Oh, and in case anyone wonders, I carry a puppy between my legs because I have to keep my knees apart and a cuddly pup is slightly more fun than a rolled-up towel or cushion.

My last two Facebook posts just focused on the positive things in the wake of Rosie's death. The simple positive things too like birds singing and the sun shining. I felt so emotionally broken I was seeking comfort in just the simplest of things. I would get through this, I knew I would. I get through anything I am thrown, but I was feeling pretty battered and bruised. I knew I needed to be gentle on myself and allow myself time to heal. I needed to take comfort in any little thing I could to make myself strong again.

November 2015

1st November 11:42

I'm the luckiest person on our ward because not only do I have my hands but I also have this view from my bed! Such a beautiful day again and I can hear the birds singing too! I can't actually get up though and go outside as I still need help with my brace, but do you know it's absolutely blissful lying here just listening to the birds' happy chorus, especially the robins as there are quite a few of them. Watching the wind rustle the golden coloured leaves on the trees I feel very content.

2nd November

Monday morning can always be a bit ropey wherever you are and this morning started a bit wobbly here. St David's Ward was short-staffed. I had rowing first thing and I love that more than anything! Unfortunately there were no members of staff to help me get my brace and clothes on so I decided to try and do my best on my own. I turned up fifteen minutes late, really upset as I was sure I'd missed my turn, and needless to say rather dishevelled. To my delight my physio said she could squeeze me in! I was even happier to beat my last time of how quickly I could row 500 metres by 42 seconds, a personal best! I may look like I've been dragged through a hedge backwards, but boy I have a massive smile on my face.

22:04

I'm trying to organise a special birthday treat for my Megan's eighteenth birthday party and wondered if anyone had a marquee I could borrow? Obviously I won't be the one putting it up though.

Being in hospital in some ways was quite nice. I had no real responsibilities. I had all my meals brought to me. I had everything organised. It was a safe little bubble where I could escape from the harsh realities of the big world outside. Unfortunately, being in hospital for a significant period of time also meant that you could miss out on special events that were going on in that big world outside. Meggie's eighteenth birthday was at the end of November. I was already starting to think of how I could make it a day to remember from my hospital bed. I didn't want to disappoint her or let her down but I already knew it wasn't going to be how I would ideally like it to be. I was learning since my accident that things don't always go how we want them to, but that we have to make the best of what we have. To worry about things we can do nothing about is wasted energy. Our energy is so important and we should try to only use it positively. I would do the best I could and concentrate my energy into my rehab and getting home again. That, in the long run, would be the best present I could hope to give.

3rd November

I started the day thinking it was Wednesday not Tuesday and ended up going to a class I didn't have, and accusing some poor woman of taking my turn on the exercise bike! Ooops. I did apologise profusely. I then found a spare five minutes to pluck my eyebrows but then actually felt quite sad when my ward neighbour, who can't use her hands, said she'd love to be able to do hers. I just assumed she had bushy  eyebrows by choice! I offered but she said if she let me loose on them I'd talk so much that I'd forget to stop and she'd have none left, so bushy was a better option! My favourite nurse took me out for a special treat tonight in her own free time, she is just the nicest most caring nurse ever! We went to Wagamamas – I'd never been before and we used chopsticks and I managed to flick a noodle onto the table next to us. I think they thought my action was due to me being in a wheelchair – little did they know I was like that before my accident!

4th November

Good morning, I'm excited! Hopefully today I will have good news. I'm expecting a lumber spine scan today which will inform me that my vertebra is completely mended and at long last my 'beautiful' brace can come off!

18:38

I so wanted to post a happy smiley no-brace picture today but alas no! I had three scans in the end, an X-ray, an ultra-sound and the all-important CT for my back. I got the results for the first two but not the one I really wanted. I missed my first haircut appointment as a consequence and I so desperately need a haircut! I think subconsciously I took my frustration out in table tennis this afternoon. Every poor patient got hit by my balls, even those playing on the table next to me, and even the visitors helping to collect all the balls got caught in the line of fire! Needless to say I won't be entering the Paralympics as a GBR table tennis player!

5th November

OK, so Miss Positive here being positive, giving an update on the brace. Firstly, the good news is that I have a lovely straight spine. The bad news is that my break was a really nasty one as I think we know, and some of the bones still don't look like they have fused together. The surgeons and consultant and his registrar are meeting on Monday to discuss whether the bones have mended enough for it to come off, or if it needs to stay on longer. Apparently it can take six months for the bones to heal! On the bright side, yes it's pretty painful and very restricting and not overly attractive, but it enables me to get up out of bed and move around and have fun! I had fun today and even did some Christmas shopping for my babies. Oh, and I've struck a deal with my consultant: if I have to keep it on for six months they are spraying it pink.

6th November

Bert and Ernie have started to get a little too naughty lately and on a couple of occasions have nearly thrown me out of my chair! Today when I went to sit in it they locked straight and wouldn't bend. This sort of behaviour sometimes happens and is caused by strong muscle spasms. One way of stopping this is to have lots of physio and keep them moving, or otherwise to inject them with Botox as this paralyses the muscles thus preventing spasms. I think it's funny that Bert and Ernie might get beauty treatment lots of women pay good money for!

Every spinal injury is unique just like the person the injury has affected. Some people get spasms, some people don't. Everyone also deals with their injury in a unique way. I have friends who hate their spasms and take medication to stop them. Some have or are awaiting Botox injections. These paralyse the muscle and stop the spasms. I have many mixed feelings and emotions regarding these. They make me think that my legs still have life in them and to stop them would feel like killing my legs. I like them moving. I know that I will never walk again. I have accepted that quite happily and moved on, but when they move it reassures me that actually they aren't broken or damaged. I know it's just that the messages from the brain aren't getting to them any more like they used to.

7th November
It's blowing a hoolie outside and the rain is lashing against the window but I'm a happy bunny sitting on my bed 'embracing' my brace and really looking forward to seeing my brother and family later!

8th November
Some say things in life always happen for a reason and I'm a firm believer in that. My accident happened for a reason, several reasons in fact I think! Today I met up with friends I haven't seen in years and years, we bought soup, bread, cheese and ham and my friends had brought homemade lemon drizzle cake and flapjacks. We sat and talked and laughed and ate like no time had elapsed at all. Then three more friends joined the happy throng! I ate so much I thought my brace would burst and just thought how an accident can bring people closer together to enjoy really happy times. If that's not a good reason for it happening I don't know what is!

Friends meant so, so much to me before my accident but even more so since it happened. I think it is possible to get through any challenge in life with a good network of strong, caring friends by your side. I had the support of so many lovely people who helped keep me strong. Meeting up with friends from primary school taught me that good solid friendships can stand the test of time and are there when you really need them.

9th November

I am certainly a walking disaster or should I say 'wheeling' disaster!! I got the news back today regarding my brace. I am going to need further surgery on my back as the break hasn't mended. It is still very weak and needs more reinforcing. I have no idea when or exactly what. They like to keep you guessing here, but apparently I have been offered a psychiatrist! That made me laugh. It's just another challenge to get through I guess, and I'm already making sure I get as fit as I can so I can recover quickly to get home. Rosie dog's ashes came home today and I want to come home too.

20:01

A proper cup of Yorkshire tea, not made in a blue plastic cup with a straw makes EVERYTHING better!

I think that November was one of the hardest months at Stoke Mandeville psychologically. Everything in my life had become so unstable. I had lost my old boy cat Diesel. Then Rosie had died just a week later and now I needed another big operation. Was it not enough that I had suffered a pretty horrific accident and would never walk again or run and cycle or lead the same full-on 100-mile-an-hour life that I had led. I felt that I had dealt with everything so well and yet still it kept coming, more 'crap' to deal with. I was starting to wonder if my luck would ever change, so again I dug even deeper than I thought possible to dig and carried on with that positivity that had served me so well up to now.

10th November

A couple of weeks ago the lady in the bed next to me went home and I miss her terribly. I now have a lovely lady, a little older than me, as my neighbour. She is having such a rough time at the moment though and I really feel for her. Despite this, she has a fantastic sense of humour and we have become very fond of each other. She has very limited movement in her hands but is so determined to do as much as she can herself and I've kind of become her little helper! Tonight she had a dysreflexia attack, her third one in just over a week, and I hate it as it can cause a stroke. I just have to wait outside closed curtains until it's over. It makes me quite anxious and emotional. Today she missed her tea as a result, so I made her Weetabix and toast and marmalade. We laughed as she kept dripping Weetabix all over her sheet, she told me off for putting too much milk in the bowl and I said next time she could flipping make her own! I sat by her bed and we held hands for ages. Her hands really hurt and it helps if I rub them. We were just relieved she was well again. Then she let me eat all her Lindt luxury chocolates.

Whilst at Stoke I formed some very intense friendships very quickly. I think this is because everyone is in the same boat and you cling to each other for comfort, understanding and support. Very sadly, though, some of these friendships dissolve as quickly as they are formed when you leave hospital. The friends you make in hospital come and go. Often there is quite a distance between you when you get home. Dealing with getting back to normality with your new disability can be very, very difficult to come to terms with and friendships just seem to evaporate.

11th November

Such a happy Wednesday morning commencing with hydro, jacuzzi and of course the shower from heaven. I then received some lovely news from my brother Adrian in Ireland. He organised an art exhibition to raise money for me and my pink wheelchair. An article was published in the local Irish paper about the exhibition and my accident. A group of Derry runners saw the article and contacted my brother and said they'd like to raise money too and have organised a running event this Saturday! Isn't it just so amazing how kind-hearted people can be  and they don't even know who I am. They just want to help regardless! I feel very loved today and have a big smile on my face.

19:42

Such a fantastic day. I managed a whole minute's silence at 11am and thought of all the soldiers who lost their limbs and ended up in wheelchairs so we could remain free, as well as those who died. I got treated to a lovely lunch and travelled by car, still such a new and exciting experience. I got to smell a bonfire today too, that sounds ridiculous but I LOVED IT!

I got a haircut and received loads of presents today. I also saw a beautiful canine partner dog called Elliot and had a good cry and have more friends visiting later. I have no idea when my surgery is but I know I will be bed bound again for some time and I will be going up to the high-dependency unit. I am therefore making the most of my independence and freedom before it goes again, but I know I will be just as determined to get it back.

12th November

A day of firsts today. I was allowed to lay on my tummy for the first time since the accident and managed forty press-ups, which I was so pleased with. I think my hard work in the gym is paying off. I also had my first ride on a handbike; what a laugh it was riding along the hospital corridors on that. I had the best time ever!

13th November

I didn't realise but my physio recorded this! I had a go on another handbike today too, a real racing one. My accident hasn't put me off my love of speed, and it may be Friday 13th but I had some good news – Mr Blagg, who is carrying out my fixation surgery, is coming to see me on Monday.

20:44

One of the hardest things to deal with has been to accept the deterioration of the appearance of my legs. Like the majority of us women I like my legs silky smooth and this has practically been non-existent in here. I can't bend to shave them myself with my broken back and surprisingly

enough they are not on the list of the nurses' priorities. Initially it bothered me loads looking down at 'men's legs' and skinny puny, no longer toned ones at that – and hence the name Bert and Ernie! I would feel quite anxious and embarrassed especially going to hydro with them in such a state and feel very self-conscious! But do you know something, no one in here actually cares about them and we have a good old joke about them constantly. Tonight though I was determined to do something about them, so I attempted to sort myself out in the shower! Now they look worse than ever as I could only manage to reach patches wearing my brace. I gave up after one leg as my brace was hurting too much when I bent down, but do you know something, when I go to hydro again or the gym no one will care what they look like! In this place people really do value the beauty that comes from within.

14th November

I think the tragedy in France has affected millions of people today. I know it has had an impact on me. It has made me appreciate even more how lucky I am to have such a beautiful family when so many people's families have been destroyed. I miss my gorgeous children every day but I have the reassurance in knowing that they are safe and surrounded by love. They are such a credit to me and make me immensely proud. Each week that I see them, they have grown stronger and more amazing in my absence. I cherish them more than life itself.

22:52

On a more light-hearted note, Bert and Ernie got a full haircut today by a nurse in the shower. There were bargaining terms of course and the condition was that I didn't say a word for the rest of the morning! Drastic measures were taken to ensure this and a pillow case was shoved in my mouth!

Having my legs shaved today was not really about appearance. I have already mentioned in an earlier post that hairy legs are not frowned upon here as there are much more important things to be concerned about. It was for how it made me feel mentally. It is so important to try and not let your appearance slip because it helps you hold everything together. You need to be in control of all that you can control. This is because of everything you have lost. The importance of cleaning teeth, washing and shaving legs was not about appearance but preserving mental sanity.

Teeth cleaning used to cause grief with the nurses at times especially if they were busy, but I cleaned them religiously first thing in the morning and last thing at night. You could almost see them sparkle across the ward!

15th November

Family time is so, so precious I felt very privileged to be taken out for lunch with a very special family today! I also had a really special experience back in the hospital as well. I am under no illusion that I will ever walk again, but my feet were experiencing a lot of neuropathic pain when we got back to the ward. My friend gave them a good rub to try and ease the pain. When her husband held my feet I could feel his hands were warmer than hers. It's not an overly big thing but anything to me is a bonus. I am grateful for any little sensation because I know I damaged my cord so badly and should not be able to feel anything.

16th November

So, so tired. I have been anxious and waiting all day for news regarding my surgery. Finally, Mr Blagg has just been to see me. The procedure itself is pretty clever but also quite complex and will take about half a day. The date will be 9th December unless a slot becomes available beforehand, but the best news of all is I have been promised I can come home for Christmas!!

17th November

I woke up this morning feeling pretty grumpy and sorry for myself. Originally Christmas was my date to come home and stay home permanently. I was feeling quite disheartened and disappointed that as a result of further necessary surgery I have to return here again afterwards for more rehab. Plus I got stuck between the shower chair and bed last night when a transfer went wrong and it made me realise how vulnerable I am without the use of my legs. I needed a nurse to help lift me out of my predicament and help me back to bed. I had two choices – stay in bed and mope or get up! I got up and rowed, I went on the NuStep bike, a bit like a cross trainer for those whose legs don't work, and stood in the standing frame for almost an hour. To finish off I practised some of the most difficult transfers from one bed across to another bed with great success, and do you know what? I completely forgot how miserable I'd been in the morning and how lucky I am and how much I have to look forward to and enjoy.

18th November
Now I have the facts regarding my surgery clear in my head I can share them with those who would like to know. It's quite a long read, but I think it's a very clever thing they are going to do. A piece of bone is going to be taken from my pelvic bone. It will then be inserted into the gap in my vertebrae that hasn't fused together. For this to happen one of my discs will be removed first and hopefully the new bone will fuse the two vertebrae together like cement. Extra metal work will also be added as well as this, attaching the two separated vertebrae. This is in case the added bone doesn't work. The metal will do the job of my brace so at last the brace can go. The work is being done to the front of my vertebrae. To carry out this type of surgery my chest cavity will be opened and a lung deflated, a chest drain will then be added to drain off any excess fluid and air and will remain in for twenty-four hours after surgery.

Finding out about my second operation was a completely daunting experience. I could scarcely take it all in, it gave me such an anxious tummy. A lot of people would choose not to find out exactly what is entailed but I wanted to know every last gory detail. I was very worried and scared as I knew it was going to be such a big set-back. Ultimately though it was the only way forward, so I knew really there was no choice.

19th November
I'm feeling a little chuffed with myself this morning, I've taught Bert and Ernie a new party trick! If I squeeze the back of my knee it makes the toe next to my big toe wiggle up and down. Ernie is a quick learner and responds really well every time but I think Bert needs a slap because he is lazy. I think maybe he is even a bit slow as he tends to take his time to co-operate but he gets there in the end.

20th November
Today we were shown a manouevre called a scoop to help right yourself

in the event of a backwards tip in your wheelchair. Much more fun in the gym with pillows and a crash mat than the real thing though, I think!

Lots of transfers we were shown in the gym were very possible within the security of the four walls and soft padded mats, under the supervision and assistance of the physios. Putting them into practice in the big wide world was a totally different matter. This fact actually played a massive role in my decision to discharge myself a month early. I was fed up playing at being disabled, I wanted to get out and do it for real. Boy what an eye-opener that turned out to be!

21st November

Lots of beautiful pictures and posts have already been added to Facebook, but I had such a truly amazing and memorable time today with some great friends, family and very inspirational people! I completed my first 5k since my accident with a man called Ben Smith. He is running 401 marathons in 401 days without a break, raising money to support anti-bullying initiatives. Such an incredibly humble and selfless man

who was so interested in hearing all about other people, I was buzzing when he left. It was freezing cold today but high spirits kept us warm. I've also signed up for my first marathon as a wheelchair-bound person in October in Bristol. This will be Ben's 401st and I can't think of a better marathon to start with.

Meeting Ben Smith whilst in hospital had a real impact on me. What a truly memorable experience and what a totally selfless, beautiful man. He left me feeling so positive about everything even with the prospect of a big operation looming that was playing heavy on my mind. This was one of my best days in rehab and one I truly would cherish.

22nd November

Ben posted a beautiful picture on his 401 challenge Facebook page last night. I made it my profile picture. I love it so much, not because it's me as I actually still find it hard to comprehend pictures of me in my chair. I quite often think I still have the use of my legs, but it doesn't matter whatever your shape, form or ability is – if you want to do something you can. Running is one of the nicest ways to bring people together from all different areas of life and I think I will run for ever in whatever shape or form until I wear myself out completely.

23:44

I had a bit of an ordeal in the shower but I'm now feeling happy in bed as I've been scrolling through my Facebook feeds. I've also had a day of surprise visitors. Firstly, from Gary the man who rescued me back in August and his partner Zena Warwick. It's always lovely when Gary visits as I always think back to that fated day and wonder what would have happened had he just cycled by. I sometimes wonder when I see him if he actually would still have stopped had he known how much I talked. He assures me he had quite a good idea as I was doing a fair amount of chatting when lying in the bushes! I also had a lovely visit from Ben Smith this evening who had just finished yet another marathon! He had framed some of the pictures from yesterday including the black and white one that I love. I was so excited, to say the least, and even managed to bounce on my bed without toppling over! I really wanted to go back down on the track, too. My journey is such an exciting one and my life is nothing like I thought it would be but I wouldn't change it. I've met such lovely people on the way and have such supportive, caring friends, and I haven't even left hospital yet!

23rd November

Monday is an exciting day and between 2pm and 3pm everyone who has Mr Saif as their consultant loiters around their beds. We are all waiting for him to come and discuss our health and progress. Today the main topic of discussion is my surgery. Apparently between now and the 9th December I have to wrap myself in cotton wool and not catch any cough or cold or bug that could impede my operation. I don't think he was overly impressed with my antics on Saturday outside in freezing conditions in three-quarter-length capri running bottoms. Also I'm having an X-ray as I may have somehow chipped a bone in my foot. At least it doesn't hurt though! There is also talk of not being well enough to come home for Christmas post-surgery, but hey, if I can't go home for Christmas, we can just bring Christmas here instead. I'm feeling very happy today, but I was told by my physio when I was giggling through our weight session, that even when I cry I still smile.

24th November

There are no expenses spared at Stoke. I even have my own special wash bowl with my name on it! I'm not the best in the morning at getting up; in fact I'm a right lazy bones! I continuously wake up and then doze off again and quite often miss breakfast. I blame it on the lying down thing. Not being able to sit up in bed makes me sleepy. I'm also completely helpless, and useless without my brace on and rely totally on the nurses anyway. I'm lying here now with my bowl of hot water procrastinating and looking at Facebook when really I should be getting up.

Mornings at Stoke were a real struggle. Invariably St David's was always short-staffed and very disorganised. It wasn't their fault, so staff and patients were both frustrated. There were classes in the gym that many of us missed because there were not enough staff to get us there on time. I used to get very disheartened with this fact but what could I do? I used to try and blot it out by just going back to sleep. Then quite often I missed breakfast too. I remember one morning in particular getting up early while the night staff were still on duty to have a shower. Sometimes it was easier for night staff to do this as they had more time before they went home. I came back to bed and fell asleep again. It was all completely chaotic as the day staff had just started their shift and I wanted to escape it. When I awoke I had missed breakfast. I still could not sit up without my brace so I wriggled like a little worm down to the end of my bed where I had a bag of nuts. I was really hungry and started munching on them for breakfast. At this point a member of the day staff decided to open my curtains. They were still shut as I was naked after my shower. I was still naked but now I was also upside down in my bed munching on a bag of almonds. The nurse most certainly didn't expect the sight she received. She just laughed. 'Oh Amanda, I never know what to expect from you. You just always make me laugh.' Some days that is what you had to do. You had to laugh and make light of things or otherwise you would end up really miserable and depressed and there was no way I wanted that.

25th November

Lying here reminiscing how eighteen years ago this beautiful lady was only three hours old and lying in my arms! I've watched her grow from that tiny bundle of helplessness into the strong, determined and independent woman she has now become! I hope she knows just how proud of her I am today and always and how much I will think of her on this very special day! Megan Worne I love you with every single beat of my heart and cherish you today and always! HAPPY, HAPPY 18TH BIRTHDAY MY GORGEOUS GIRL XXX

00:30

Today I felt a bit wobbly about being apart from my baby girl on her eighteenth birthday. Meg soon pushed all those wobbles away as she showed me how amazing and strong she is! All day she has sent me pictures and updates of what she has been doing and I have been able to see for myself that she has had a truly wonderful day. We chatted on FaceTime too and I saw her blow out her candles on her cake. I also saw all the beautiful presents she got from her lovely friends. I have felt a big part of her special day today even though I have been miles away and as I go to sleep I feel very close to my Birthday Girl, too! Love certainly conquers all.

It did feel very sad and strange not being home to welcome Meggie with a big birthday hug as she came into the bedroom in the morning before school to open her presents. Not being able to sit on the bed with her as we sung happy birthday, especially as it was her eighteenth, made me very sad. I really had a genuine ache in my heart and it wasn't the healing ribs. It really is only when you have things taken from you that you completely realise how much you take for granted. I know Meggie tried her hardest to make me feel included on her special day but I knew that it must have been very hard for her, too. It was days like this that gave me the deep and strong determination to get through my rehab, have this second, stupid operation and just get home to be with my family again.

26th November

Thirteen days to go until surgery and, oh yes, I'm counting. Such a truly fantastic afternoon supposedly just nipping into Aylesbury for an hour's shopping that turned into four hours due to the start of Christmas late-night shopping. I bought quite a lot of Christmas bits and bobs, which Debs Pacey had to carry as I couldn't balance it all on my chair. We got stuck in mud trying to take a short cut on the way back and I laughed so hard my brace nearly burst! Every day is special and I really am blessed that I have had an experience that really makes me realise that. I also want to store up some fun times to help see me over the bed-bound days after surgery. They will also give me the incentive to get well quickly so I can enjoy some more.

27th November

Fantastic Friday. I walked!!

> I used the statement 'I walked' very loosely in my post. I was and I'm still not under any false illusion that I will ever walk again. I hold on to a little hope that I may possibly be given some new treatment in years to come that will repair the messages in my spinal cord, but again I don't realistically think that there will be a cure in my lifetime. I am happy with what I have, happier in fact than I have ever been. I used the equipment in the gym that helped me move in an upright position because that is what I was actually doing, to give me a good cardio workout, to aid my digestive system and also help my circulation. My accident had a massive impact on the workings of my body. I want to help maintain what I have now the best I can. We only have one body and I want to look after it. My accident taught me that it isn't indestructible so I treasure what I have and want it to be in good working order for as long as it can.

28th November

A lovely day spending a belated eighteenth birthday with a beautiful young lady!

> Today was never going to be easy and it was never going to be exactly how I wanted it to be. I had organised a small surprise party for Meg with just family and close friends. We set up a room we had hired with balloons and banners. A lovely friend had given me a beautiful penguin birthday cake as Meg loved penguins, and that had pride of place in the

middle of the table. Another friend had also supplied a couple of beautiful cakes and other friends had made sandwiches and other savoury dishes. It was just lovely to all be together. My brother from Ireland flew over and I think that was the best surprise of all for Meg. I had a lot going on in my head but just for a couple of hours I could put it all behind me. Today was Megan's day and I just concentrated on making it as happy and special for her as I could.

29th November

Sunday in the runners calendar is a day when many racing events are organised. People race for many reasons, maybe an attempt for a personal best, for charity or for fun, and of course earning that bit of 'bling'. Whatever the reason, it does still, and I think always will, pull at my heart strings. I simply loved my Sunday races. I'm optimistic that after surgery and once the weather gets warmer I will get my racing chair and be able to join in once again. Instead today I went to Asda and bought fluffy socks because my feet are getting sore from the bed and need protecting. I have a blister on Bert's toe which could take up to three weeks to heal because of the change in circulation to my legs, so I don't really want any more. Oh, and today for the first time I got called a spastic; it was meant in a 'nice' way. The man using it genuinely thought that's what I am – it's funny because it made me feel quite strange and I guess it hurt. I still feel like I'm me, I haven't changed! I know I am different now but I find it hard being labelled or put into a box. I guess I just want to be called Mandy and feel normal and I think from being here that's what the majority of people think too.

30th November

Good Monday morning! A new week and a new timetable. It's like being back at school and I get a new one every week. All showered and dressed and sitting on the bed drinking tea and eating salt and sweet popcorn for breakfast. Yum yum!

17:59

Another great day and another day closer to surgery. A volunteer visitor insisted on doing my hair today and I didn't have the heart to take it out but I think she thought I was five! I managed the hardest transfer of all today, the transfers of all transfer in physio! I managed to get myself onto the floor from my chair and then back up into it again. I was the only one in my group who could do it as well, and Bert and Ernie keep fighting with each other, so we've had to get Ted to intervene and keep them apart!

The lovely volunteer lady came round our ward every Monday. She was an Irish lady and always very happy and bubbly. She talked incessantly about her grandson and it was obvious she adored him. When I first came onto David's ward she used to walk past my bed and just smile hello. Then she used to come and have a chat when I had been on the ward for a bit longer. The first time she came over to me I mentioned my four children. She was gobsmacked. With all my cuddly toys and pink blankets and Hello Kitty balloon she had thought I was but a child myself. I don't think her perception of me ever changed though, as was evident today with the lovely hair-do.

December 2015

1st December

I can't deny that with just a week to go, surgery is very much on my mind. Even my consultant said today he can't wait until it's over! I had a release date of 23rd December to come home for good (I may have already said). I'd kept it as a surprise from everyone and I'm disappointed that isn't happening. It was my Christmas present to my family! A really sweet friend cooked me a lovely plate of fresh vegetables in garlic and tomato, which tasted amazing. Hospital food drives us all mad day after day and she knows I'm anxious about things. I had a blast in the gym, though, on the rowing machine with the GBR team. Not that I'm competitive or anything, but I beat everyone with the same injury level as me. I managed 97 metres in 30 seconds and I said I'd be back after my op to get 100 metres. It lifted my spirits no end, it's important to end the day on a good note!

2nd December
I've had a really lovely day! I had my first 'proper' haircut hospital style. I also had a really good fun physio session with Sylvia, a lovely Polish girl who fell down a cliff on holiday in Spain. We had to try and throw balls in boxes behind each other but also try and block each other's shots. Balls flew around the gym left, right and centre and quite a few other patients ended up getting involved. We sat around the kitchen table afterwards and drank honey tea which Sylvia introduced me to, and as true wheelie friends, Sylvia helped me put my slippers on because she can bend further than me as I have my brace. This time next week, though, it will be gone!

3rd December
A really fun-filled day! I helped an older friend compose and write her letter to Canine Partners and then took it out to post. I loved seeing her so happy as she has had a rough time lately. I visited the Christmas fair and met Yaris, a Canine Partner dog, and watched him in action. He

was amazing. Lovely friends from Australia visited and they put Christmas lights on my chair! I felt like a big kid, I was so excited! Finally, another visit from a friend with whom I practised bed yoga and whose fingers I felt tickle Ernie with my eyes shut. I'm collecting so many happy pre-op memories.

I've debated getting a K9 partner or assistance dog, but I feel that I would be robbing someone else of the chance as I am quite capable of training my own dog. Other people have a greater need for one of these dogs than I and I could see that looking at my lovely friend as she cried when she read the letter I had composed to Canine Partners.

4th December

Just a little story I thought I'd share. I've been blessed to meet many amazing people since my accident. Yesterday I met a girl who left a huge impact on me and really made me count my blessings. She was selling handmade crafts at the Christmas fair and had an adorable working dog with her. I asked her how long she waited to get a dog and she replied that due to mental-health issues she was fast-tracked and they got her dog after only five months. It normally takes two years. This got me thinking and I wondered what her circumstances were. I went off but returned later for another fuss of her dog and of course another chat! I asked her if she didn't mind telling me how she became wheelchair bound. I didn't expect the answer I received. She told me as a teenager she tried to commit suicide and jumped off a bridge. She landed on her feet and succeeded in breaking both legs and paralysing herself from the waist down. She spent her first one and a half months lying in a full body brace flat on her back staring at a ceiling in a hospital. I was stunned! I told her it was a blessing that she had survived because she was a very special young lady as she was so kind letting me fuss her dog and cuddle him, as many owners of assistance dogs don't allow their dogs to be petted. I told her spending time with her and her dog had made my day and how many smiles she had put on so many faces visiting her stall, chatting to her and again fussing her beautiful dog. It materialised she had made all her crafts herself and was now also a wheelchair dancing coach. She said she still had low days but at those times she snuggled up to her dog and just stroked his ears. I purchased several items from her and she gave me a little Christmas tree as a keepsake. Maybe I will never see her again but I will always remember her and how she hit the lowest point I think anyone could reach but turned herself around, and with a lot of determination and courage she has achieved so much.

5th December

I worked hard today in the gym and walked in my robot machine further and faster and still had energy left for fifty press-ups! I was then taken out to lunch by two lovely friends but not before I faced my most challenging car transfer to date. It was all the way up into a Land Rover. It was worth the effort though for a delicious lunch in great company. I also bumped into Mr Blagg, my surgeon, and he assured me we still had our date on Wednesday! I'm desperate for the day to come now as I feel the strongest and fittest since I've arrived. I'm hoping all the hard work will pay off on the big day.

23:32

I spent a very lovely afternoon with the most special people in my life today. These four brave, amazing people keep me going and keep me strong! I have to blink twice sometimes when I look at them to take in the fact that they are my flesh and blood, my children! I won't see them now until after my surgery and saying goodbye was tougher than ever tonight, but I can't wait to hug them all properly without my hard black brace. It turns out, too, that they are all quite good shots with a rifle as well, so the surgeon had better do a good job and mend me good and proper.

I know I continuously talk about my children, but to me they really are my world. I truly believe that it was because of them I fought to stay alive in those bushes for over half an hour. It was because of them I had the strength to keep overcoming every obstacle that came my way. It was because of them I got out of bed every day. I was more worried about my surgery because of the impact it was going to have on them. I knew I was going to be quite poorly and weak again afterwards. I just wished it didn't have to happen, not for my sake but for their's. It meant the end of days with the brace and as I wrote in my post, proper squidgy cuddles again. I knew it was the right thing to do.

6th December

Today the fairies decorated my home and this evening I saw all the beautiful decorations on FaceTime. Jacob down-loaded and sent me a CD of all our favourite Christmas songs we played when my children were little. I had a fairy here today who helped me buy and decorate my own Christmas tree so I could join in the fun. I cannot tell a lie though, I really would much rather be sitting at home snuggled on the sofa with a small Baileys on ice watching a Christmas film with the pretty lights twinkling and all my family around me!

Putting up a tree in my room made me feel more connected to my family at home. The fairies always used to come when the children were asleep and in the morning when they woke up they would come downstairs to a Santa's grotto. I can see their little sleepy faces now with big wide sparkly eyes trying to take in all the decorations around them. It was magical. Christmas meant so much to us as a family and this year was going to be very hard for us all. I wanted to make the best of my Christmas in hospital. It seemed only right that if my home had a tree up, then I also had a tree up. I felt it was important for my children to see that I had entered the Christmas spirit, too, and I was excited about them coming up to see it.

Oh happy Monday morning! Already I've missed my last hydro lesson for quite a while and been told my Christmas tree is an infection risk and I have to take it down. I only wanted the children to see it when they came up. I had put chocolate Santas on it for them too. What can I do though, lie and cry about it or just smile, take a deep breath and say 'Hey ho!' Either way the situation stays the same, so I'm saying hey ho and smiling – I'm sure the day will get much better. I'll just have to make sure it does.

The housekeeper came and took my tree down. I cried. It had meant so much to me putting it up. I put the chocolates that I had hung on it for my children back in my drawer. I would give them these when they came up to visit. I only had a couple more days down here anyway until I had to go back upstairs to the HDU where I knew I would put it up again. Everything was a struggle at the moment. This was just one more thing and in the grand scheme of things it was actually very trivial. I had much more to worry about, as surgery was getting closer and closer.

8th December

I'm dealing with tomorrow like a big race. I've 'carbed up' like I would do before a race and I've done all the training I can do. I now just have to approach the 'start line' with a positive mental attitude as I would before I race. I know it's going to be unpleasant and I will be out of my comfort zone in a very big way. I have an anxious tummy already but I know the surgery will give me so many benefits. That is what I must focus on. I have a badly broken back that won't mend and without tomorrow I will have to wear my painful restricting brace for ever, so what more can I say than let's get this race started!

9th December

Nothing like keeping me on my toes. Yesterday I was told surgery was after lunch so I could have breakfast. I went and bought bagels – yum yum! I got woken at midnight and informed I was second on the list so their were no bagels, but I could drink. I am woken at 7am to be all cleaned up and suited and booted in my lovely theatre gown. I'm told nothing at all and to be ready to go down at anytime. They know I'm a bit cheeky so the nurses have confiscated my water bottle and have even taken my advent calendar in case I eat all the chocolate! They have also given me a lovely sign so I don't try and trick some some poor unsuspecting nurse! I bet I'm still here at 2pm (Sylvia and I cooked a special last supper together. It was just delicious but I don't envy the anaesthetist with the amount of garlic in it).

10:48

Thank you for all my lovely messages and support. I am such a really, really lucky, lucky lady – I never believed I could be loved so much by so many! Surgery will be a breeze with everyone wishing me well and it will be quite apparent when I go off to theatre as I will go quiet on Facebook.

17:47

Oh dear – I'm really sorry but I've had everyone on tender hooks all day and I have just been told my operation has been cancelled. Mr Blagg, my surgeon, came up to see me. He still wanted to do the op but the administrators wouldn't give him the staff. He looked genuinely disappointed for me and so apologetic I really felt for him. He wants to try again for Friday, but it's not looking hopeful either – the NHS are really struggling and it is taking its toll on its staff. I've spent a whole day in bed with no food or water since tea time last night and I'm starving! I am disappointed but I guess it will happen when it happens! So the brace remains for a little while longer.

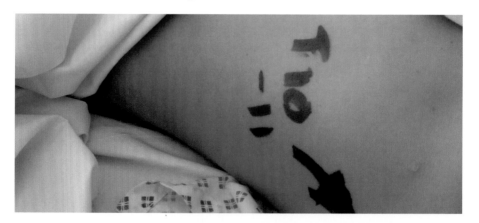

Today was nothing less than mental torture. To be drawn on marking the location of the surgery, gowned up and all prepared ready to go, only to hang around in bed all day. I was unable to eat and watched all the other patients go off with staff into Aylsbury to do their Christmas shopping. I

was missing out on this because of the pending surgery. I probably felt the lowest I had since the day of my accident. I also started to get impatient. I asked a nurse to phone theatre at about 4pm to see what was going on. She got no reply, so I googled the number and phoned myself. Mr Blagg was still in theatre. He had started late that morning. I just knew my operation wasn't going to happen. I actually didn't care, I was past caring and just wanted to eat. At about 5pm Mr Blagg came up to see me. He looked so tired and more disappointed than I felt. I could tell he was very upset that he had let me down. This just made me feel sad for him. It wasn't his fault. I hate seeing people sad so I told him not to worry. I told him it was obviously not meant to be today after all, and that all I wanted now was a hot buttered bagel. I knew he would do his best to get me another date as quickly as possible and I trusted him. He left and five minutes later, low and behold, a hot buttered bagel appeared!

10th December

I've had a productive day today all round. I did ten laps of the track in my chair and a lap of the gym in the walking frame. This was to make up for being in bed all day yesterday. While I was out I was informed that my surgeon had popped into the ward several times himself rather than getting his secretary to phone, to tell the nurses of his plans for my surgery. They said he seemed very, very intent on doing it as quickly as he could and was very concerned about me, which was lovely to hear! I am lying in bed tonight feeling tired but happy and positive that things will all be sorted out very soon.

I took all my frustrations out today in the form of exercise. I had heard from Mr Blagg and surgery was scheduled for the next day. This was my last day of freedom and by God after yesterday I was going to enjoy it.

11th December

I didn't want to worry or disappoint anyone again so I didn't post that I was having surgery this morning and although I look pissed as a fart and can hardly stay awake, I am actually the HAPPIEST lady alive right now! Surgery was a complete success and

I am FREE! The brace is a thing of the past and the future couldn't be brighter!

> As I have said, I hate people being upset or disappointed so I didn't tell anyone I was having surgery in case it was cancelled again. I had met my anaesthetist the night before and we got on like a house on fire. He too was a fellow triathlete. I was down in theatre by 9am and we were chatting again as he prepared to put me to sleep. Mr Blagg said hi and was wearing a pink hat for surgery. Apparently he always wore blue but heard I liked pink. I was all ready to go. I was talking nineteen to the dozen to Rich, who was the anaesthetist, all about life, my accident and my family. I just remember him saying that he thought, and these were his exact words, that I was 'fucking awesome'. He then put me to sleep and I'm sure that was when he probably thought I was even more awesome as I had certainly given his ears a good bashing and was finally quiet!

12th December

The first day towards finally going home is almost over. I had a tough night with an hour of absolutely no pain relief as it didn't kick in and I've never known pain like it. Not even in the bramble bushes back in August. On the plus side, I now have morphine at the touch of a button which I can press every five minutes. This afternoon my chest drain also came out – whoop, whoop! I also have a tube that goes into my side providing me with a block of anaesthetic internally to help with pain, too! I lost a lot of blood and my magnesium is low so I have another line going into me containing magnesium which filters in over eight hours. I've also had intravenous antibiotics and I'm on oxygen. I'm being monitored very carefully every two hours as my blood pressure is also very low. I know I'm in good hands but it will be some time until I'm back on my feet again, or should I say in my chair. This time, however, it will be with no brace and I will be wheeling myself out of the hospital door – I can't wait!

13th December

Looking slightly less drunk than Friday night I think. I've been able to catch up on a bit more sleep today. Last night I was woken at 11.30pm for an X-ray and again twice hourly for turns and observations. Two more drains have come out today and another four X-rays taken. One will hopefully confirm the brace can come off! I'm pretty bored flat on my back again, so am open to anyone who fancies a visit. I've been lucky though, and lots of nurses and patients and family have come in over the weekend.

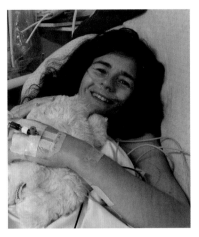

14th December

The photo proof that the brace can finally come off. To be honest, however, today was a struggle. Everyone is keen to get me mobilised again, but we are struggling to get the pain relief under control. I've had a few occasions today where I didn't know what to do with myself. I've hurt so much. My breathing isn't regulating as well as it should either, and I'm still on oxygen. I have a lovely team of nurses working tonight so I'm hoping for a positive day tomorrow. I'm trying to remember just little steps and be patient.

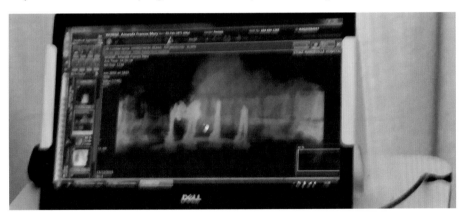

It's only reflecting on these above posts that I realise just how much the second lot of surgery took out of me. I think if I had been given that type of operation when I first arrived in August it would have killed me. I have never felt so poorly or been in so much pain in my whole life. I don't really even remember Vic and the children visiting me the day after. I know I kept trying to stay awake but I kept falling asleep. Apparently in the car on the way home they all moaned what a blooming wasted journey that was. It had most certainly knocked the stuffing out of me.

15th December

Good Tuesday morning! I'm feeling much happier and much brighter today! The pain relief team are really working and getting on top of this, so I'm much more comfortable as I'm getting strong, regular doses. I know so many nurses, staff and patients here now and I've had a constant supply of people popping in to say hello, which has been really uplifting. Not sure if I will get up later. I really want to wear my Christmas jumper without my brace covering it and to start feeling a little festive. My oxygen levels are still low, though. It can't be because I'm talking too much – I'm actually being really quiet at the moment! Everyone is quite shocked. I'm sure it won't last so they should make the most of the peace.

20:52

My Christmas picture in my Christmas jumper by the tree, brace-free! Just need my family now.

16th December

Last year I watched Joe's nativity performance in Arundel Cathedral. Who would have ever imagined I would be watching a hospital Christmas show in my hospital bed today, well that's just what I did! A beautiful little show put on by caring, lovely hospital staff devoting their free time to give their patients some Christmas joy. There were nibbles, and Brian who is a patient played his violin while we sung carols. The staff performed some hilarious dance routines and if I could have given a standing ovation I would have.

I just felt so awful today. The thought of having to get in my wheelchair to go and watch the Christmas show reduced me to tears. Luckily for me I had a friend visiting and she fought my corner. I was giving myself a hard time and not coping that well on this particular day. We had a really lovely chat and put the world to rights. She is a nurse and could tell I was

feeling peaky and said I should stay in bed and get the nurses to wheel me down, and she saw to it that they did. It was also funny as this friend leads a very busy life and just popped up the once to visit, but she came at a time when I really needed her. This happens in life sometimes – people just kind of appear when you need them most. I will always remember this day and always be grateful.

17th December

AMAZINGLY POSITIVE DAY in many ways! I got out of a blood test – oh yes! I had homemade pizza for breakfast – yum! I went to the gym NOT IN MY BED, IN MY CHAIR, and did half an hour practising sitting without my brace. I stayed in my chair for TWO AND HALF HOURS! I was allowed to put my tree up and FATHER CHRISTMAS – the real, genuine one because I tugged his beard! – BROUGHT ME A GIFT to put under it. A package of mince pies and clotted cream arrived in the post too – proper, proper clotted cream! I felt so happy I even had a hug with my brace as I felt sorry for it all alone in the cupboard. To top it all I phoned home and Jacob Worne got amazing results in his GCSEs under amazing stress and pressure at having to deal with me being here!

18th December

Even after four and a bit months I'm still getting lovely cards in the post and Christmas cards too. It keeps me smiling. I also learnt today that there is 'no room at the inn' on David's ward so Christmas on Andrew's ward it is!

19th December

Had a visit from my oldest and youngest and I certainly know how to live it up. While everyone on Facebook is out Christmas partying I went to Asda for the first time since my operation. I have to say I used to come home from a Christmas party less tired than I did from Asda today! Just over a week since my big operation and it literally knocked the stuffing out of me. I feel like I'm getting there slowly but it has been a much bigger battle mentally this time round. I think this happy-go-lucky lady almost met her match – but not quite!

22:06

The angels of Christmas really are looking after me and I am so happy I could cry. An hour ago I was told I was moving to Patrick's ward as an emergency had come in. I felt my eyes fill with tears. I'd just got settled and found my feet on this ward again and this was my home for Christmas. Alas, it appeared not to be. Half an hour later I find myself in a twin bedroom with the bed by the window. My room mate turns out to be one of the loveliest people you could possibly meet, although she is home for the weekend. So I find I have a room to myself and grinning like the cat that got the cream. I have the window open with a cool fresh breeze blowing through on my face. My lilies are opening and I can just smell their fragrance and I am drinking cold tea through a straw, and pain level is zero! At this precise moment life really doesn't get much better as far as I'm concerned.

20th December

Eating hot white toast with REAL butter in my NEW ROOM and loving my life!

21st December

I really can feel I am gradually getting my strength back and turning a corner. Today I transferred in the gym without my sliding board. I also sat upright for almost an hour but did have to hold on to the bench when I started to feel sick. I feel so, so alive at the moment, where everything is mending. The body is such an amazing machine. I am very blessed with the body I have after all that it has been through and it is still so willing to try its best for me. Humans really are amazing beings!

The feeling of finally getting back to half human again was second to none. This operation was much worse than the initial accident in August. I don't think my poor body knew what had hit it and had completely shut down. Yet again, though, she still came through for me in the end. It is just unbeleievable how much we can cope with and how the body fights so hard to keep us alive.

22nd December

Whilst chatting in my room last night to my roomie, Kerri, we were suddenly interrupted by the beautiful sound of magical bells. Kerri ran outside to see what was going on. An ensemble of bell ringers had gathered outside the door and were playing Christmas carols. I was desperate to see, so Kerri unplugged my bed and wheeled me outside. Time stood still for about twenty minutes as I listened to the magical sound. My stay at Stoke Mandeville has made me realise how much effort people make at Christmas time in hospitals, spreading goodwill and cheer to the patients and ensuring they have a lovely Christmas, too. It was a moment I will cherish for ever.

23rd December

I've been suffering with a bit of backache (funny that) in my chair without my brace as all my muscles are adjusting to having to support themselves after four months. Today in the gym my physio gave my back a really good stretch and OMG what a difference it made! I did six hours in my chair today and felt much better and even cooked my dinner. Sylvia managed to drop a whole bag of tangerines in the lift as the door opened and a couple got stuck on the door runners. We couldn't stop laughing as I can't bend to pick them up at the moment and she had to hold the door open so that they didn't get squashed. We had to wait until a walker came by and rescued us! I'm lying in bed and can hear the nurses playing Connect 4. My roomie has gone home for Christmas and I have the whole room to myself. Christmas is almost here!

Looking back I did have some really good fun during my stay at Stoke Mandeville. I think that is because I chose to make it that way. We are in control of our own happiness. Happiness does not come from things or people around us, it ultimately comes from within. We make our own happiness and I am fortunate to have the ability to even make a sad situation into a happy one. Things just need flipping on their heads sometimes and I have the mental ability to do that. I thank God on a daily basis for this precious gift.

24th December

What a brilliant Christmas Eve. Lots of FaceTime with my children at home and I've been well looked after all day by just the most lovely staff EVER! I'm about to have my first Indian since the accident with two beautiful friends, which could end in disaster, but it's Christmas and finally I've set the nurses a challenge. They are going to pretend to be Santa and see if they can manage to sneak all the presents I've been so generously sent into a pillowcase at the end of my bed without waking me! This is a tradition I had as a child. The challenge has been accepted. I'm feeling quite excited and I know I'll try and stay awake. I feel like such a child all over again!

21:35

I have a feeling I'm a very lucky lady with lots of lovely friends! I would love to reply to each and every one of my beautiful messages, but I will be awake all night and then Santa won't visit me! Feeling very, very loved. Thank you all so, so much!

I mentioned a curry I had ending in disaster. Potentially, eating spicy food increased the likelihood of a bowel accident. Low and behold I had one Christmas Eve. Since my surgery I was back to bowel emptying on the bed, which was never very successful for me before and was proving that way again now. It was embarrassing as it happened when my friends were with me. They were lovely and just left the room while I was sorted out, but even though I know it's not my fault it still makes you feel very embarrassed and degraded. It is also something you can't dwell on though, you just have to put it behind you and keep moving forward. 'Shit happens', you just had to deal with it, and I think it was the hardest thing I was learning to deal with.

25th December

I just want to wish everyone a truly special and magical Christmas from

Stoke Mandeville. Enjoy and treasure every moment as I truly intend to do, too!

20:26

Bert and Ernie weren't entering the Christmas spirit this morning and weren't too keen to get out of bed. They put up a bit of a fight but I was having none of it as my lovely nurse had promised me my first shower in two weeks. She spoilt me rotten today – I had an hour long Christmas shower! She is an absolute angel and is away from her family, too. There were carols around the ward again with lots of patients and staff joining in. Mum and Dad joined me and brought Christmas dinner and presents, lots of beautiful presents.

The first time I've been alone with them on Christmas Day in forty years. I sat on my bed unaided with no brace for the first time today, too. I'm alone now, I've FaceTimed, phoned and texted home many times today. Obviously I have missed my family as they are my world, but we've all had a lovely day in our own little worlds and are so looking forward to the best day ever together tomorrow.

Christmas Day, and the most poignant thing I will remember and will remain with me for ever is yet again pooing myself in my pretty party dress. The Indian from the night before had taken effect. I had had my first shower and hair wash since my operation two weeks before. It was the best Christmas present ever. The nurses helping me took off their shoes and socks and rolled up their trousers and did a little dance for me and I was naughty and sprayed the shower on them. We were in the shower room for almost an hour and what a brilliant time we had. I'd just sat back on my bed after Christmas dinner and low and behold I could smell that ominous smell. I called a nurse, my parents left the room and I just cried. I could not believe it had happened on Christmas Day. To top it all, the nurses had real trouble getting my dress over my head without getting poo in my nice clean freshly washed hair. So I cried more than ever. But do you know what? It didn't kill me, no one was hurt and my mum took the dress home and washed it and brought it back as good as new. It also resulted in the nurses deciding to put me back on to Peristeen as soon as possible to try and get my bowels back into some kind of routine again. I will always remember the Christmas Day I pooed in my party dress, but I'm sure I'm not the first and I imagine I won't be the last. I haven't really touched on bowel treatment and how bowel care is managed by a spinal patient long-term. I was having a lot of accidents with my bowels, which I was finding really upsetting and actually harder to deal with than not being able to walk. The bowels are a part of the human body that are very hard to train, mine were certainly proving that for sure. One lovely nurse took pity on my regular accidents when I was on David's ward. She knew how positive I was being and how I loved being active and she could see how my bowels were restricting me and bringing me down. For this reason she introduced me to Peristeen, which is an anal irrigation system. A lot of patients manually evacuate their bowels, which just gets rid of poo in the rectum and needs to be done every day. It was what the nurses had been doing for me on the bed early in the mornings. Now I was mobile I needed to start thinking about emptying my bowels myself. The manual evacuation was not reliable enough for me because it was not clearing enough of my system out. I needed something more thorough and this is what Peristeen would give me. With Peristeen, water is flushed into the lower colon and poo is removed from here as well as just inside the rectum. It would give me a longer period of time before it built up again, giving me more security and less chance of accidents. Hey presto, it worked! The accidents stopped and at last I felt really confident in being able to trust my bowels without the same risk of them letting me down. I could really start to enjoy being active again. Peristeen had proven to be a life-saver!

26th December

Ooooooh how excited am I – my family on their way! Bert and Ernie are doing the fandango!
18:22.
The best Christmas present a mum could ever have. The moment I've waited for all Christmas.

Today was supposed to be the best day ever. It started off a complete disaster. The children were all awkward when they arrived and everyone seemed to be in such a bad mood. It was an alien situation for all of us and none of us knew how to act. The key to the hospital bungalow had gone missing. We were using the hospital bungalow to give us some real family time. We finally found the key. There were no decorations and it was freezing cold. To top it all I had forgotten to close the flip-flow valve on my catheter, which meant all the wee in my bladder leaked out because the tube wasn't attached to the bag. I was soaked. I had to go back up to the hospital and change. Again, I cried. It seemed to be all I was doing at the moment. I just felt that I was such a failure and disappointment to my children. I wanted today to be so, so special and it was just a complete nightmare. When I got back to the bungalow, presents had been laid out and the heating had warmed the place up. Things were looking a lot brighter and the children had perked up a bit, too. Today was about being together as a family through thick and thin, good and bad. We were all safe and warm and that was what really mattered. Only a few months earlier it could all have been so different and I felt truly blessed to be there with them all.

27th December

I awoke this morning a little anxious that I would feel very flat after seeing the children yesterday, but today turned out pretty OK. I almost sent a friend in her chair crashing into a glass door backwards. I gave her a book to look at and it rested on her wheelchair controls! I also performed a real labour of love – I am a real reformed non-smoker and helped a girl have a cigarette. I put it in her mouth, lit it and flicked the ash for her. It literally made my toes curl, but I could see she really enjoyed it! I had to wash my hands so much after to get rid of the smell. Finally, I have formed a really lovely bond with my anaesthetist. He visited me for the first few days to check I was OK and then phoned Christmas Eve to say he would pop in today. Indeed he did, right in the middle of when I was sitting on the throne! He wasn't put off and had a very bizarre conversation with me through the partitioning curtain. I really couldn't believe it – a chat over coffee would have been nicer I think!

Helping my friend smoke her cigarette means even more to me now. I recently learned that she died of a heart attack. She leaves behind her four young children. Life is so cruel sometimes. Hearing the news upset me greatly, but she was more seriously injured than me and suffered greatly with lots of spinal-related issues. At least now she is at peace and can watch over her babies from above.

28th December

New year, new start, anyone looking to get fit? I have a cross-trainer that I think I may have difficulty in using now. If anyone is interested please message me. I paid £250 for it and it is quite a big robust one. I am open to any offers and whatever I receive I'm putting towards my new pink racing chair.

21:01

The week between Christmas and New Year can be a funny old time but I had such a lovely day today. I was pampered this morning by a nurse who

painted my nails and straightened my hair. I had some lovely visitors bringing beautiful flowers and Ernie got to meet the real Ernie. I was also really touched by the man on the till in the café. I was waiting for my chips at the buffet counter and he came over to me asking if I wanted to pay while I waited. He took my money and returned with my change saying he had only charged me staff rates on account of my beautiful smile. How lovely was that! I'm getting much faster again in my chair and my operation wounds are healing well. The year 2015 is going to end on a very good note, I think.

29th December

A busy, busy day today with a good stretch in the gym to begin and then lots of lovely visitors. I had my first venture out into the big wide world without my brace. I did actually feel quite exposed! We took a stroll down to a pub a good mile away and I did have to have a push as I'm still healing and building up my strength. On the way back it was a bit chilly and my knees got ever so cold. We got back at 5pm and a nurse has just felt them and they are still cold now at 9.30pm! I'm also quite excited as I have received a letter inviting me to participate in the Interspinal Unit Games in April. I really consider this invitation a big honour and hope I am able to attend.

30th December

When you have one of your closest friends from your school days visit you from the other side of the world you have to make an effort and try and stand for the occasion!! High on Thorntons toffee I stood for half an hour and didn't pause for a breath once. Annabelle May and I had a lot of catching up to do!

It's amazing what good company can help you achieve. I found that when I used to run it was much easier with someone just plodding along chatting away. The miles would just go by and this was the same.

31st December

Lots of people are making New Year's resolutions and setting goals for 2016. Deep down I find it all quite overwhelming, apparently that's quite common though, due to my accident. I have little dreams in my head regarding 2016 and get excited thinking about them, but in all seriousness I can't think much further forward than what today might bring, let alone a year. That isn't really so bad though, as I can really only guarantee that I have today anyway. All I wish for is to continue to be surrounded by my beautiful family and network of such strong, caring, amazing friends who have been such a support for me over the past few months. I treasure this more than anything else. I really don't need legs with the loving people I have in my life because they give me wings. I am the luckiest person alive and wish everyone a happy, happy New Year!

10:15

OH MY GOODNESS GRACIOUS ME! I can hardly contain my happiness. I started on Andrew's ward, then George's, David's next, back up to Andrew's and a visit to Patrick's!! I've just literally been told I'M OFF TO JOSEPH'S ON SUNDAY! That is my final destination before I go home. I finally have my ticket out of here starting on Sunday!

> *I think sometimes people put too much pressure on themselves at New Year. We make resolutions and after a few days we are already breaking them. I didn't put any pressure on myself whilst in hospital, I would take each day as it came. It's good to set goals and challenges but I think it is human nature to be too hard on ourselves and expect too much. It's far healthier and mentally easier to try and live each day the best we can and not to focus too far ahead.*

January 2016

1st January

Yawn, stretch, Happy New Year's Day! Well I certainly know how to see the New Year in like a real party animal! I had to have two bed changes as I managed to sit on a bag of anaesthetic fluid used for my surgery wounds and it leaked everywhere. Then I managed to flick a whole beaker over myself whilst moving my bed covers! I toasted the New Year in with a nurse with a cup of 'Laxido' – now that's novel! The highlight of the evening was quite special and moving. During the first night after my surgery a beautiful nurse cared for me. That night was a bit of a haze due to all the drugs, but I remember her sitting at the foot of my bed watching over me. She turned me every two hours and arranged my sheets and blankets, did my observations every four hours checked all my tubes weren't blocked and even gently woke me to tell me to breathe properly when my sats dipped a bit low. She came in to me as Big Ben struck twelve and we had a big hug and shared a few tears. This year I'm hoping to go from strength to strength and rebuild my life back at home, but I will cherish my many memories in hospital and last night was certainly one of them.

2nd January

I have been given a standing frame of my very own to take home with me. Humans were meant to stand upright on two legs and although I can't do this on my own any more it is still very important that I do. It aids my circulation, regulates blood pressure and strengthens bones. Most importantly to me though, it enables me to hug my precious children in the most natural way I can. My first stand-up hug in five months!

3rd January

I can honestly say hand on heart that I have never once felt bitter or angry about my accident and thought why me? I actually think it's good that it ended up being me as it has hopefully saved someone else from this fate. Maybe another person, a little less happy-go-lucky than me, wouldn't cope as well. My goodness though, the luck I have had since has been amazing! Today I moved to Joseph's ward and well, it might as well have been the Ritz! I have the best room in the spinal unit, the only one with a bath, a flipping bath I tell you, I was so, so happy! I feel like I could fly. My rehab will be much easier with such a beautiful room. I'm trying to calm down and take things slowly but at the moment I have so much excitement and energy I could burst!

4th January

Doh – I should have guessed it was too good to be true. A patient with MRSA type 'B' has been admitted; theoretically this beautiful room is for patients with infection or who are pregnant. The sister in charge is making a decision whether she can leave me in here and put her new patient somewhere else. I may be moving AGAIN already! I really hope I can stay but I can fully appreciate it if I can't!

22:03

Phew. I'm still in my penthouse suite but I'm still not certain for how long. Life on St Joseph's is very, very hard. It sounds pretty feeble but I'm managing to shower and dress myself completely independently. It takes so long – I never knew putting on a pair of trousers sitting in a wheelchair could be so much hard work. To top it all I flooded the bathroom too, water crept all the way out to my bed. I was completely oblivious to the whole thing as I was struggling to slide back to my chair across a board whilst soaking wet. Lucky for me my occupational therapist turned up and we had a mammoth mop-up session – well, I sat and watched and made unhelpful comments! I had the best lunch ever with my little bro who helped make a warm avocado, bacon, Brie and mushroom salad. The smell of cooking bacon attracted the attention of everyone on the ward still suffering under the hospital food menu. I made a return trip to Patrick's ward to rescue half a cucumber from their fridge and was welcomed like the prodigal son! I'm so lucky that I have friends everywhere now. I'm a little apprehensive about tomorrow, as again the challenges are much bigger down here, but will just take things in my 'stride'. One thing is sure: I will sleep so well tonight.

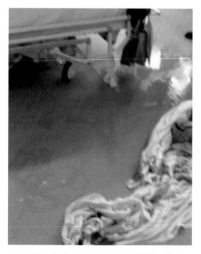

Coming down on to Joseph's ward was a big shock to the system and I hated it. It was so quiet. I felt isolated and alone. I was basically just left to my own devices and after being upstairs where there was lots of hustle and bustle and someone always popping in to see me, Joseph's ward was just the opposite. I could have rung for help if I really needed it, but because I had been given such a lovely room I felt I couldn't ring as I would be letting people down. I didn't want to fail so I wanted to be as independent as possible quickly. This was extremely hard though. I had been through major surgery just three weeks before so I was still sore and healing. I would get my independence back but as I was learning so much on this journey I just needed to give myself time and be a little patient. Easier said than done.

5th January
Guess whose coming home for the weekend...

To be told that I could go home for a visit was better than any news I could possibly receive. After all this time I really could see getting my life back a reality, not just something I dreamt about. The final stage of rehab was really beginning and with it came a surge of emotions. The hardest, most fulfilling stage of my journey that I was on was about to begin.

6th January

I've had a roller-coaster of emotions today. I had such a lovely visit from a friend. We worked together at Pizza Express many moons ago, so we paid a visit to our old haunt in the Aylesbury branch. We had an attentive waiter who said I could keep the hat and scarf worn by the pepper pot. I've got a few issues, though, that need sorting out; they will plague me for the rest of my life but I won't go into graphic detail about them. I'm struggling with them at the moment. Tonight is also my last night in my room. I'm moving tomorrow so I'm feeling a little unsettled and if I'm totally honest I'm feeling really homesick and can't wait for Friday.

7th January

Well the day started with a really horrid procedure that knocked the stuffing out of me and I've felt ropey all day, but I was determined not to let it get me down and I had such a lovely time this evening it made this morning seem like a bad dream. Nothing special, nothing exciting, just wheeling round the hospital with my Ironman buddy causing trouble and laughing. We put a request on the hospital radio channel. We requested 'Firestarter' by The Prodigy, but it was refused because of being offensive to the burns unit. We couldn't help it, but we cracked up laughing – all running, walking related songs are allowed, it just made us laugh why this one particular song wasn't (maybe someone will enlighten me). We also barged in on a hydrotherapy lesson with half a dozen people being very serious exercising in the water and were asked to leave! We spent so much time laughing, my sides hurt. And finally I've moved rooms, but the exciting thing is my old room is occupied by a spinal pregnant lady who is having a caesarean tomorrow, how exciting is that! We are going to have a newborn baby on our ward.

It's not something that many of us feel comfortable talking about, but as a spinal patient I was learning that we all talked about our bowels very openly, especially at the meal table! As a spinal patient our bowels can give us so much trouble and dominate our lives. I also feel it is important to share with people so that they get more of an insight into what people with spinal injuries really experience. Since my second operation my bowels had been all over the place. As the prospect of coming home became more real I was really anxious about getting them sorted out. At present I was suffering from really bad constipation. This morning it had become so bad that I was going to have an enema. Not the nicest of experiences but necessary to sort me out. Oh my goodness, no wonder I felt so bunged up. When the enema took effect there was no stopping me. The nurse who was carrying out the procedure was gobsmacked. Every time she thought I had finished I started again producing more and more. I think she actually felt sorry for me; to be full up with that much waste, I must have felt really uncomfortable, and I really did. When she came to writing up the notes, as bowel movements have to be recorded, she put 'a massive bowel movement'. To be precise almost two large orange disposal bags full!! I felt quite rough after the experience too. I was really learning how dangerous being seriously constipated could be. Potentially it can kill you and as a spinal patient it is so important to keep on top of it. Getting these bowels sorted was crucial and it was playing heavily on my mind.

8th January

In the car eating yum yum's and listening to the Muppets song on the radio. Almost home and so excited!

22:37

Apparently the Jackpot on the lottery tomorrow is 60 million pounds! I've won the Jackpot already as far as I'm concerned: five months in a hospital bed and tonight I sleep in my own bed surrounded by the people I love the most. Life doesn't get any better than being with the ones you love!

9th January

A very, very special Saturday morning from me in my own bed. Pain is truly controlled a lot by the mind. I have had a strong morphine-based painkiller every night at about 2am in hospital since I can remember. A night in my own bed and I don't need it! I've woken up feeling the happiest and luckiest person in the world. Last time I woke up from this bed and went out I never came back. No one knows what is going to happen to them, they really, truly don't. Today I am going to really cherish every moment.

The feeling of sleeping in my own bed is one I will never forget. Everything around me was familiar with familiar smells as well. Nothing could compare to that moment. I didn't feel scared at all being out of hospital. I felt I was where I should be and it gave me more determination than ever to come home for good.

10th January

Having such a lovely time I don't want to go back, so I'm staying here for another night. Home sweet home!

I found a small red mark on my bottom and didn't want to risk sitting on it all the way back to Stoke Mandeville in case I made it worse. I phoned them and told them of my concern and low and behold I was allowed to stay home for another night. I was secretly hoping that would be the answer and was made up when it was.

11th January

Finally, able to kiss all my children goodbye and send them off on their way to school again. Plus, this long awaited for moment, seeing with my own eyes how handsome this young man looks in his new secondary school uniform. I missed out on his first day due to my accident. Going back to Stoke will be very hard for me today. I really feel ready to come home. There are many challenges ahead – I've witnessed that over the weekend, but I can't achieve them from a hospital sanctuary. It's almost time to start my new life and journey.

14:50

Arrived back and I've already told everyone I'm going home for good asap. Oh, and heard the cries of a newborn baby in my old room!

12th January

Today I have achieved my biggest and by far my hardest achievement. I certainly WON'T be allowed home until this goal is completely mastered. I bet if I asked how many times you spent a penny today you would probably have to think about it for a minute. Today I have spent the whole day trying to just spend one single penny! I have to monitor how much I drink when I drink, and how long between each spend. And it took me about twenty minutes to go! I have never been so determined in my life to master my new art of penny spending because if I couldn't do it the way I now do, I would need a tube inserted in through my tummy and into my bladder. Something I've never really thought about before has become such a priority and poignant part of my life. I am relieved I've mastered the daytime habit but I now have night-time to contend with too.

21:04

A challenging day calls for a bit of fun to finish the day off. I met an amazing girl who has entered the Paralympics twice as a hand cyclist and this year she is rowing in Rio. Hopefully she is going to help me choose a handbike. I got to career around the gym and up the corridor on a specially adapted Segway and I managed not to crash or fall off!

The joys of self-catheterisation. I have already mentioned this in my past reflections. Now I was ready to try it for myself. Lying on your bed trying to keep your legs apart when they want to spasm shut, balancing a mirror in between them so you can see where to insert the catheter because you can't feel anything, and then actually trying to insert a catheter somewhere that is completely alien to you – not an easy procedure. Learning to self-catheterise on the bed comes first. The catheter is attached to a little bag. When you finish you can rip the little bag open and empty the contents into the toilet. As you progress you learn to insert a catheter whilst sitting on the toilet. It is just a little tube without a bag and the wee goes straight into the loo. I couldn't really think this far ahead. Self-catheterising was a massive challenge and I was just breaking it right down and taking it one step at a time. It was another step closer to home.

13th January

Simply the best day EVER! It's almost five weeks ago that I had my surgery. Today in my goal-planning meeting my discharge date was finally decided. A date of 23rd February had been pencilled in but I have been absolutely desperate to be home for good on my birthday on 2nd February. Often a discharge date is changed, usually to a later date. Today a discharge date was changed but it was brought forward. My date was changed to 29th January, two weeks on Friday. All the hard work has paid off, I am just BURSTING WITH EXCITEMENT – IN SIXTEEN DAYS I COME HOME FOR GOOD!

To be told I could go home a month earlier was just the sweetest music to my ears. All my hard work, all the surgery, all the pain, all the tears and all the emotional ups and downs had been worth it. In two weeks I would be back home for good.

14th January

Brilliant day with lots of laughs. Woken up to be told I could go to hydro as someone had cancelled. My first since surgery. I was told to be quick and get 'a wiggle on', which made me chuckle as that is about all I can do these days without my chair. I received a mysterious box seemingly full of wine gums, yet to my great delight it turned out to be a Hello Kitty blanket, which was lovely especially as the weather has turned colder. I visited my friends on all the other wards and found some of them all very merry and Rosie cheekily drinking a smuggled bottle of spicy rum, one of my favourite drinks, so I joined them for a quick sneaky tipple. I'm now at the services on the M25 getting hot chocolate and looking forward to a few more days at home. All good practice for two weeks' time when I do it for real.

15th January

During my stay at Stoke Mandeville I have 'played' at being less able-bodied; everything is geared up for the likes of me and wheelchair people are the majority! There is always help at hand and a nurse is just a red buzzer away. There are no red buzzers outside Stoke Mandeville for me to press for help. Real life is geared more for the majority of able-bodied people, not for the wheelchair bound like me. This is where the role-play ends and I really start to learn what it feels like to be a person with a spinal cord injury. I'm going to meet the challenge face on. It may sound silly or strange, but I am looking forward to my new life ahead of me and both the ups and downs it brings and the adventures it holds.

16th January

It's just a little idea but I have been so lucky to have so many friends supporting me on my recovery journey that I thought maybe on Sunday 7th February I will be at the Maypole in Yapton, which is local to me. Anyone who wanted to come along and say hi between about 7 and 10pm could pop in and join me for a drink. I hope this sounds OK as it is a way for me to say hello and thank you in person to people who have been there for me along the way.

18:49

Lovely to be drinking in a 'local pub' and then actually being able to return to the comfort and warmth of my own home and the smiling faces of my beautiful children to welcome me, and to then share a family meal together. Feeling so blessed and truly happy.

17th January

So far my home visits have brought to my attention that:
1) Baths are disastrous as I float clean off the inflatable bath chair and nearly drown.

2) The chairlift from the top down is a death trap and I've fallen off twice.
3) I can get out of the house independently but I can't shut the doors behind me.
4) Once outside and the door is shut I can't get in again.
5) I CAN have a shower
6) I CAN reach the work surfaces.

Lots of things still need doing, which is why I have weekend visits to discover what I can and cannot do. The most important thing is that I CAN spend time with my family. Back at Stoke now and how nice to come back and find someone else in my room and for me to have moved yet again. I'm back in my posh room with the ensuite bathroom – I wonder how long for this time?

> *Each time I had a weekend visit, coming back to Stoke got harder. It used to be my little sanctuary, my little safety bubble, but now it felt like a prison. It was holding me back, keeping me from my loved ones and preventing me from living my life. I felt that in a way I was betraying the hospital after all it had given me, but I knew it was good for me to feel like this. I knew that my time at Stoke had come to an end. It had given me all I needed but now it was time to move on. I was more than ready to go home.*

18th January
Lying on my tummy for the first time since surgery without my brace. It's called lying 'prone'. I'm not sure why, but where I sit scrunched up all day it stretches out my back and hip flexes. I hurt all over now but it's because I'm not used to it. I just have to practise more. I chatted to a charity today about possibly going skiing in Colorado next February and

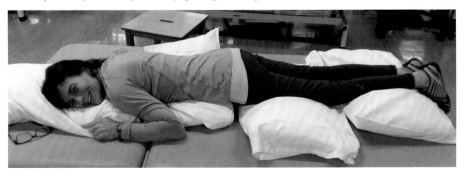

an outdoor activity week this summer – there is so much available out there it's amazing! Having something exciting to look forward to really helps with the day-to-day challenges for sure.

19th January

I've been following all the running, cycling and fitness posts of friends on Facebook daily. Today for the first time since surgery I got outside for some fitness myself. It felt amazing and so invigorating especially as it was so fresh and cold with the beautiful winter sunshine. A national handbike champion has started working in the gym on a Tuesday, so we went down on the track and he recorded a 3km distance on Strava. He made me work so hard and even when my broken rib popped he showed no mercy! I've certainly learnt in here that things like broken ribs and collar bones, sprains and pulled muscles do not count as 'injuries'. Broken backs, people on ventilators and with tubes everywhere are the people with real injuries. Strength of character is certainly tested. This place has made me a lot stronger I think, but then I will need to be pretty strong to face the challenges when I come home in just ten days. I certainly feel ready and I just can't wait!

20th January

Found myself being dragged along to a presentation night on motor racing. I thought I'd be bored stiff. How wrong was I! The most unbelievable lady told her story of how she came by her injury (a car crash at sixteen years old) and where it led her. She is called Natalie McGloin and she is the only female tetraplegic racing driver in the world. I was really moved by her journey and I'm hoping to visit a racing track she is setting up later in the year to race in a Golf GTI; she races in a Porsche 911! To qualify for her racing-driver status she had to be able to get out of her car in 7 seconds. I think she will help me overcome my fear I've developed of going fast. I've been a little anxious about this fear but she has told me five months after my accident is still very early days and I will eventually get my confidence back again. I am so pleased I went.

21st January

Another day of firsts today. I stood for the first time in heels, much to the shock horror of the physio's – it would be so easy to snap my ankles if I went over in them, but there's nothing like wearing a pair of heels, so it's a risk worth taking! I also came home via Bury Hill tonight and became reacquainted with an old friendly signpost but think my brambles have disappeared. Tonight is the last dummy run home. Next time it will be for good.

22nd January

It's cold, wet and miserable outside but the sun is beaming down on me today. I got a letter confirming my place for the Stoke Mandeville Inter-spinal Games. Only eight places on the team so I feel absolutely proud as punch to be chosen. I just need to start training now to prove I'm worthy.

23rd January

I haven't mentioned it before but it has been quite tough coming home and not being welcomed by a big happy, waggy tail from my Rosie. The house feels a little empty without her. Animals are intuitive though – Abby Tabby my cat has never been overly affectionate and in all her twelve years she has never jumped up on my lap. Since my accident things have changed. Today I bent down to stroke her but am unable to pick her up for a cuddle. The next thing I knew she jumped up onto my lap. It really made me feel quite emotional and ever so happy. I love my animals so much. I have chuckled a few times since my visits home - I've bent down to stroke a cat without looking, only to realise I'm stroking my fluffy slippers!!

24th January

I was presented with a lovely breakfast this morning. I'm going to have to be careful if these continue, as I'll get fat! I have lots of exercises from Stoke to carry on maintaining tone and movement in my legs when I am discharged. I spent half an hour or so doing those today, then half an hour lying on my tummy and then standing in my frame. I really have to look after my body more than ever these days as so many complications can develop if I don't. A nurse

told me that prior to World War II and in underdeveloped countries one of the highest causes of death in spinal patients is pressure sores. Tomorrow I have a visit from the occupational therapist with an 'overlay' mattress to put on my normal mattress to help with that. I also spent an hour playing the piano, or attempting to – it gave me brainache, the first real mental stimulation since August. Due to the accident trauma I haven't even read a book. I've attempted to and just skimmed pages. Thank God I finished my degree in June.

25th January

Back at Stoke for the last time – just four more sleeps to go, but it was tough coming back today. I know it's only until Friday but that feels like for ever. Back and forth between Stoke and home makes everything disjointed and unsettled. I just can't wait to make the journey home for the last time.

26th January

I've noticed recently that my knees have been clicking on and off when I bend them. On asking my consultant what this meant he said it was most possibly due to the waste of muscle around the knee. The knee caps and surrounding area are not supported any more so will slip in and out of place more easily. I remember how I had a knee issue on my first marathon and worked so hard to strengthen them so it wouldn't happen again. It is very hard watching a major part of your body that you have done so much to maintain and look after just waste away and being helpless to stop it! I've given Bert and Ernie a good rub and massage to compensate for things I can't prevent happening, I feel very protective over their vulnerability. I'm also panicking as to how much 'stuff' I've accumulated in five months. For most people I think it would take five years to achieve this! I don't quite know where to begin but feel a removal lorry may be needed!

So many emotions whirling around inside me. I am concerned as to how I will look after and maintain my body when I get home. I am so relieved I have my standing frame so that I can stand every day. I want to try and preserve as much of my body as I can as I have lost a significant amount of its use. At Stoke all the machinery and physios are at hand just down the corridor in the gym. At home I am going to have to start a whole new fitness regime and that feels a little daunting. I have so many other issues to think about too. To be honest, it is all quite overwhelming.

27th January

Starting to clear things out today and came upon my 'box of frogs' I got for Christmas. I know I'm mad as a box of frogs but I feel my whole life is a box of jumping frogs leaping all over the place at the moment. I'm so excited with only one whole day left here, but I keep having little wobbles when something goes wrong here. It still does quite regularly and I think perhaps I should stay a bit longer. These things and other obstacles are going to get in the way when I get home. I keep telling

myself that I have the best family and network of friends a mad frog could ever wish for. It's going to be tough I know that, but I also know they will be with me the whole way to help me cope with everything. I really am so very lucky.

28th January

OMG just the BEST last day EVER! There have been a few tears especially as I completed my last few laps of the Guttman track. Lots of laughter and hugs and reminiscing on five very poignant months of my life. A few of us also got together and had pizza and watched a film. I've ended my evening with a 'Mad Mandy' classic. I took a tour of the spinal unit to say goodbye to all the night staff. I feel on quite a high and I'm very excited, so go hurtling

back to my ward and my room – only to find someone else in my bed! I've forgotten what ward I'm on in all my excitement and gone back to a room I had a few weeks ago. I guess some things will never change.

29th January

Halfway home without the prospect of a return journey looming on the horizon. Stoke Mandeville has been my home and sanctuary for five months and there have been many highs and the odd low. Today was the high of highs to end on and a complete surprise to me, too. I had my first practice at trying to walk in calipers; it's much harder than it looks but I felt invigorated and so fulfilled. I will be back until I can master it properly, that's for sure!

30th January
Bottoms up and cheers – my first Prosecco since my accident. It's just the best feeling ever to be home for good.

> *Very, very surreal being home again. I just felt at peace and complete. I knew that there were going to be loads of challenges but that didn't worry me. I just felt very safe and secure in the knowledge that I was surrounded by such a strong and supportive network of family and friends that everything would be allright.*

31st January
The day of my accident I told everyone not to be sad about my injuries and that I would continue racing in a pink wheelchair. I have since discovered racing chairs don't come cheap! Lots of kind-hearted people have been raising money for me and Mike Houston is one. He is running the Boston marathon to help fund my wheelchair. I want to thank him and everyone else for all their support.

> *I think I had deluded myself in the early days after my accident that I would be racing around in a pink chair within a few months. I had no idea how long it would take me to firstly recover from all my broken bones and secondly adapt to how my new body worked without the use of anything below my waist. Now I was back at home I also had the daunting realisation of how restricted I was and how much I needed to learn about living back in society. Friends had been so kind donating money to my 'pink wheelchair' fund that a family friend had set up, however I was now aware that a racing wheelchair was not really something I needed straight away. I didn't even have a wheelchair-accessible home. I don't want to disappoint my friends, though, by telling them that a pink racing chair may now not be something I will invest in, but it is playing on my mind a bit and I will need to say something soon.*

February 2016

1st February

A Monday morning spinal fact from the comfort of my own bed. Before I left Stoke I had some tests done to see if I had developed any increased sensation and movement in my legs. I was tested for the Babinski reflex which I have. This is a reflex found in newborn babies. If you stroke the sole of their foot the toes curl up. Many spinal injured people have quite a few similarities to newborn babies. These are in areas such as bowel, bladder, temperature control, colic and obviously walking. This is because of the central nervous system. In babies it is immature and in spinal-injured people messages don't get through due to the damage to the spinal cord. My results showed I have gone from a T10 to a T11, which is an improvement, and I'm just waiting to receive my American Spinal Injury Association score and whether I am incomplete or still complete.

2nd February

Talk about being completely overwhelmed and absolutely made to feel like the most special person in the world. I have had many messages which I need to read, cards, presents, flowers, chocolates – so many lovely things! The icing on the cake was being lifted in my chair into the conservatory to bask in the rays of the sun. I can't get out there on my own because of a big step. I've been desperate to do that since I've come home, which sounds really daft but I can't do a lot of what I used to do, so I cherish the little things I can. Today will be a day I truly cherish too. Thank you to everyone who has made it simply perfect.

3rd February

Home less than a week and I've already managed to pull the radiator off the wall! Pleased to have got out of the house before I broke anything else and worked out a route to use for marathon training. Did two miles today but I'm still reliant on friends to come and let me out. Looking forward to a second attempt at a bath later with more success than last time. I can't wait until I can do more on my own but it will take time. I have plenty of that.

4th February

It's a long post I'm afraid. I had a bit of a meltdown today where everything seemed completely overwhelming. My own personal removal ladies moved my dressing table so I could get to some of my own clothes without relying on others. It made me realise how much my little 'Mad Mandy' world of chaos needs to change. I wanted to stay in bed with the duvet pulled over my head but Jacob had parents consultation evening. This meant facing a lot of people for the first time in my chair. A challenge in itself I felt but I got up and I went. I'm glad I did. I had to fight back tears hearing how my son has excelled  himself in all areas since the beginning of term. He has gone from strength to strength in both his academic ability and mature attitude while his mum has been in hospital. My children have been amazing and who cares that I can't reach my clothes in the wardrobe or reach the sink properly to clean my teeth, I have four treasures that are beyond value and I cherish that.

Everything is so hard at home. Wheeling on carpet is hard work, trying to use the worktops to prepare things in the kitchen, getting from room to room and upstairs, and using the downstairs toilet. I am so dependent on people for help. I miss the freedom of the hospital and the space it gave me; the easy access to the gym. I have started making plans for marathon training to give me something to focus on as I can't see any improvements being made to the house in the near future. I need to channel my energies elsewhere.

6th February

A very cold blustery 'training activity', not sure if I like the term 'wheel', around the estate. Very different to the Guttman track! I can't use the pavement as there are too many bumps and drains and potholes so I use the road. I have to really look out for the cars and so far all drivers have been lovely and smiled and waved! It's not the most ideal marathon training situation but it beats sitting indoors.

My whole life at the moment is just centred around adjustment. Adjustment to everything. No longer am I with like-minded people in wheelchairs; I am with all able-bodied people. I am adjusting to my relationships I have with my friends as they are learning to adjust to my new situation. My children and I are adjusting to each other, my body is coping with new physical demands and my mental perspective is having to alter, too. It's no wonder some days you just want to stay in bed and blot everything out.

7th February

Starting to feel excited about this evening. In case anyone doesn't know I will be in the Maypole in Yapton from 7pm. Anyone who would like to, is more than welcome to pop in. I'm looking forward to seeing people I haven't seen for a while and catching up with others in a less clinical environment and not in my pyjamas with nurses buzzing around! Goodness knows what I will wear though.

11.49

Not the nicest of evenings to go out on but most certainly the nicest of evenings spent with people helping to welcome me back into the real world. Even the four-legged kind came along to welcome me home, too!

I arranged an evening for friends to come and see me at the local pub, now that I was out of hospital. Lots of people came, which was lovely and people came for all different reasons. There were a couple of people there that I didn't know too well who I think came out of curiosity. They sat very close to me just asking questions. It actually made me feel a little uncomfortable. I have not seen or heard from them since. I am quite a sensitive soul and my accident was really testing of my sensitivity towards other people. I was having to learn not to take their actions personally. In Stoke Mandeville I was given guidance on how people and friends would behave towards me and now I was putting what I had learned into practice.

8th February

My lovely daughter took me out at the weekend with her young man to feed the ducks. This made me feel very special as their time together is precious. She has just got in from school and I can hear her in the other room. Imagine how special I feel when the first thing she asks is, 'Where's mum?'

With all my friendships being put to the test and people coming to terms with my accident in a realistic way now that I was home, just being surrounded by my family was a great comfort. Although we were all being tested too and some days were hard for us to get along and get used to my new needs, I knew that the love of my husband and children was unconditional and that they would always be there for me, no matter what.

9th February

Today marked a milestone – six months since my accident. Since that day I've undergone three operations – two very major ones and one of which was quite unexpected. A graduation, a 5k with Ben Smith the 401 marathon runner, and signed up to join him in his 401st marathon, a surprise eighteenth birthday party, a hospital Christmas, walking (if very badly) in calipers and finally a discharge home! Today I almost came out of my chair whilst out on a birthday walk with Debs Pacey when my glove tassle got caught in the spoke of my wheel. Life is one roller-coaster of ups and downs, highs and lows and I am so thankful to be here to share in that and enjoy every day that I have.

10th February

What a way to start the day. I choked back tears at this sight this morning. My first visit to the sea since being in hospital. The brightness of the warming sunshine and the volume and noise of the waves was overwhelming, Mother Nature at her best.

11th February

Not so long ago I got accused of serving up 'slop'. Such a lovely feeling to be appreciated and for dinner to taste delicious.

Getting back some normality and fulfilling my role as Mum to some extent gave me a real feeling of purpose. Cooking for the children and making them happy was very important. I still needed help putting things in the oven but happy faces round the table tucking into homemade toad-in-the-hole made me feel all warm and content inside and out.

12th February

Really brilliant day today. I can't remember the last time I was pampered so much. Meggie drew a henna tattoo over my scar to make it look pretty. A delicious breakfast was made even better as I transferred out of my chair and sat at the table. The first time I've ever done that, and to top it off, a much-needed haircut. To make the day complete, the children are home and I have an entire week with them next week with no school. Today doesn't get any better.

13th February

Trying to 'civilise' the bedroom and make all my things accessible. Had quite a bit of help from one young lady who found my wedding dress and tried it on. I can't believe it fitted her so well. She looked so beautiful too. It seems only yesterday she was in a christening gown.

14th February

I have the weirdest dreams sometimes; last night I dreamt I was shopping in Chichester. I was in Boots and an old friend came up to me and starting asking me how I was, having not seen me since my accident. I told her I was doing really well and loved being home. Suddenly, shock of shocks, I realised I'd forgotten my wheelchair. OMG what was I going to do? I told her I had to dash and rush home to get it and off I ran! I've never dreamt yet of being unable to really not walk, I wonder if I ever will.

14.24

Feeling so happy and accomplished. At last I've cracked the three-mile barrier in my manual everyday chair. It's not fast and by no means pretty but it feels so good! I'm so lucky to be able to get back out there again.

15th February

I am a really lucky lady. Since I've come home from hospital I have had such overwhelming support from so many lovely people and friends. Tonight I was made to feel so special being taken out for a birthday meal by two lovely ladies. Some mornings it takes ten minutes or so just to sit up in bed if Bert and Ernie have a real spasm attack and put up a protest. That's before I've even attempted to get to the bathroom. It's having good friends and nice times with them to look forward to that spur me on, helping me get over each obstacle. A life full of friends is a full life indeed!

16th February

Have just had the best evening with an amazing lady. I am so lucky for my children to meet her too as they are really able to see how nothing is impossible when you become a wheelchair user. Rachel Morris is training for Rio in the rowing having already won a gold and bronze medal in handbiking at Beijing and London. She is up at 4.40am every day and trains three times a day, yet still found time to visit me, having only met me once in the café at Stoke Mandeville. I feel so inspired and I can't wait for us to meet up again. I'm ordering my rowing machine in the morning!

> *A visit from Rachel made me feel completely energised and invincible. She flew around my house although it is not at all wheelchair accessible. She made me believe in myself and that I would be able to achieve so much. It is so important now that I am in a wheelchair that I have contact with like-minded people to help me realise that I am not alone.*

17th February

I've been asked since I left hospital how much money has been raised so far and when am I getting my pink racing wheelchair. In answer to these questions, to date about £9,000 has been raised. I was shocked when I looked as I couldn't believe so much had been raised in such a short time. Old school friends raised money and this has gone towards a rowing machine costing £800. Important for cardiovascular exercise and strengthening my back and core. Next week I am going for a fitting for an everyday chair which could cost up to £3,000. I will be totally honest here, I want to race and I want it to be pink but having done some research, a proper 'racing' chair isn't as practical as a handbike when it comes to racing. A racing chair puts a lot more wear and tear on my shoulders, whereas a handbike uses different muscles. I need my shoulders for the rest of my life and I'm not a spring chicken any more. A racing chair also isn't as easy to use for everyday training on the road, being more track specific. A handbike is much more versatile and finally, a made-to-measure racing chair costs thousands and thousands. You get more for your money with a handbike. I'm looking at a handbike to race in rather than a chair. Before I invest in a racing bike though, I need to get the house sorted. Top of the list at the moment is a wet room as my bathroom is totally wheelchair unfriendly. I can't even shower without help getting in and out, and when I come in from training it would be nice to be able to have a nice hot shower rather than just a strip wash. Once I feel more 'at home' in my home and settled, I will look at using the money so many lovely people have raised and get back out there racing again.

Today I took the plunge and posted to my friends about how I need to spend the money they have raised for me. I had no need to worry about the reaction I would receive. All my friends want me to just be happy and content. Therefore they trust that whatever I spend my money on will be of utmost benefit to me in every way possible.

19th February

A real massive milestone today in gaining my independence. For the first time since I've been home I opened my front door. It's just little things like this that make me feel normal, well normal-ish!

Getting back in through my own front door again on my own. It might as well have been getting into Buckingham Palace, the overwhelming joy I felt at being able to open my own front door again for the first time. My accident was really giving me such a valuable lesson in appreciating little things. Never would I have thought that opening a front door could be such a massive achievement, but then never before did I ever think I would end up in a wheelchair.

20th February

Since my accident if ever I see an ambulance with flashing lights and sirens it makes my tummy flip. It became apparent today that I'm not the only one who wobbles when they see an ambulance. My youngest was waiting to be collected from football and my mum and I were late. He saw an ambulance with flashing lights and straight away thought it was me. He got his trainer to phone to find out where I was. My accident has had an impact on quite a few lives, not just mine, but I forget just how much sometimes as I'm intent on trying to sort my own life and feelings out. Today it really made me stop and think, it most certainly isn't just all about me!

It isn't all about me. Realising the impact my lateness had on Joe was a real wake-up call. We had a chat as a result as to how my accident had made him feel. He has been so brave since this whole thing started but at only twelve years old he must feel so wobbly at times. A big change in a family's life affects everyone. At least with everyone in my family, feelings were shared and all emotions were displayed. We were stronger as a result and I felt that if my children could cope with this, they would more or less be able to cope with anything else life threw at them.

22nd February

We all LOVE a Monday morning, but I've never had a Monday morning when some 'thoughtful' person has pushed my wheelchair in so tight against the chairlift rail at the bottom of the stairs I can't actually get the chairlift down! It's all character building and although at present I am sat trying to problem solve, I know I'll sort it out. If not, what does it matter if I have to spend the day upstairs. Many people experience these problems every day and worse, but I've never even realised it until now. In the grand scheme of things I'm very, very lucky and I realise that every day.

Monday mornings are hard, every morning is hard, but it is such an achievement when I get downstairs. I've had mornings that would make your toes curl. I have had to phone Vic just as he has reached work crying and asking him to come home because I have managed to spray the whole bathroom in poo! The toilet seat had slipped when I had transferred on to it and as a result all the poo had escaped out of the gap in the back. He came back not knowing where to begin. Does he tackle the bathroom first or his poo-covered wife! How many of us have a morning like that to deal with? The bathroom got a complete bleach and I got a good scrub. I cried, Vic just shook his head, but we dealt with it. It didn't beat us, we survived and we were stronger for getting through it together. A nurse told me some very wise words. The things you can't control you just have to let go, but the things you can control embrace them and control them with positivity. I can't control the odd accident but I can control how I deal with it and how it affects me and that is exactly what I do.

23rd February

A day of lots of happy smiles. The wheels are now in motion for getting a car. That will give me such a massive independence boost, I can't wait. I was treated to an afternoon cream tea with a dear friend which was more like a cream breakfast and cream dinner as well. I felt that there was a real feeling of spring in the air as we left, which also lifts spirits and makes me feel good. I have so many lovely things to look forward to. After a long winter in hospital here's to a new exciting life with the warmer weather in front of me.

24th February

I don't often post profound quotes but this is one that really rings true to me and makes my life so much easier to deal with – 'No point dwelling on yesterday or worrying about tomorrow. Today is all we have.'

25th February

This wheelchair adventure in the 'real world' just gets better and better. As I get stronger and stronger I can do more and more and my days feel closer to what they used to. Along with my mum, I went and signed all the papers for my brand spanking new car, came home and did housework and cooked dinner. Then I went and got fitted for a new wheelchair. I can also get out the shower on my own now, I just have to master getting in. I'm feeling so positive about my life. Obviously it's harder than when I had legs but it's equally just as rewarding, if not more, and I certainly appreciate things a lot more than I did. I need to be careful, though, when I peel potatoes. I've just taken off my boots and found potato peeling inside them!

26th February

Today I held an absolutely gorgeous, most smiley happy eight-month old baby for the very first time since my accident. The huge amount of responsibility was almost overwhelming! Even after having four children of my own this was a whole new experience. It felt strange with her sitting on my lap with a lap I can no longer feel. I had to really use my core to hold her steady. I think her balance was actually better than mine, although mine is getting better. I had such a lovely time with her and her family and experienced many happy memories flooding back of my four babies when they were tiny. Life just flashes by so quickly I can't believe how big and grown up they are now, but they'll be my babies for ever.

27th February

A kind invite out to take my first venture back along good old Bognor prom today and did it feel good! Hot chocolate at the Lobster Pot and a lovely time spent in great company. We had to resort to tying Bert to the chair though, as he kept misbehaving and trying to jump off. I hope I always appreciate how lucky I am and what a wonderful place I live in.

Having such lovely friends meant that I went out almost every day and did something nice. Although I knew that this type of lifestyle would not last for ever and that eventually my life would slow down and become more 'normal' again, it helped me cope in the early days and helped give me the motivation to keep pushing forward and tackle each day.

28th February

I still quite often find Sundays hard looking at all the running posts and races and I was feeling sorry for myself this morning. I find it so important when I feel like that to turn things round, so I gave myself a good kick up the backside and braved the freezing cold weather late this afternoon to watch Joe in his cup final game. I came away feeling totally exhilarated and so proud of my boy and the Rustington Otters. They played so well against an older team and although it will take ages for me to regulate my body temperature and warm up it was so worth it and has put me in such a really good mood.

I have already mentioned how my attitude to exercise had changed. I would run or cycle nearly every Sunday morning and not go to football matches. Admittedly I did the training football runs on Saturdays and Vic did the games on Sundays, but to actually watch a game itself was important for me and my children. My accident enabled me to do things I would not do if I was so fitness obsessed as I was before. I had so much to be grateful for regarding my spinal injury as it gave me a much better perspective on life and what really mattered.

29th February

Today is an ironic day. It's my official discharge date! I can't believe that I've already been home four weeks. Looking back I realise how much my body was still recovering from surgery. I struggled just getting downstairs but I would have missed some really important family events, so it's a decision I'm glad I made. Every day I get stronger. I've organised some physio and hydro classes as well, which will help my fitness. Facebook has reminded me that today is an extra day (29th February), which has really made me smile. An extra day to get even stronger and an extra day to enjoy life.

21.39

I really tried to make the most of my 'extra' day today with a walk/wheel around Chichester Marina and then some domestic duties. I really want to be able to do all I did before my accident, and I loved preparing homecooked meals for my children. This is a fairly big challenge now in a normal kitchen where I am a midget. I can't see over the top of saucepans and they are really tricky to lift. I also have to be careful opening the oven because my knees get in the way and could get burnt, and it's hard lifting heavy baking trays especially when cooking for six. Today, though, I was so pleased as I cooked toad-in-the-hole, roast potatoes and vegetables with just minimal help getting stuff in and out of the oven. Personally, that was one of my biggest achievements to date as it really made me feel like Mum again.

March 2016

March 1st

I found out that today is 'International Wheelchair Day'. It never really meant much before, I don't think I'd have given it a second thought. Now it's my life. Funny how things change! I have also had a wake-up call as to how important my arms are. I slipped doing a transfer yesterday and hurt my left shoulder, which is weak anyway due to the accident. Normally a sore shoulder is just a bit inconvenient, but to me I now only have one good limb. I've had to take it very easy today so as not to aggravate it any more, and because I also want to go out with friends tonight. I guess from time to time my shoulders will play up and hurt but it will be something I get used to and I won't let it stop me enjoying life. Chronic pain is experienced by more people than we could imagine; they just don't moan about it. I witnessed that every day during my stay in hospital.

I'm learning that having broken half my body it is so important to look after what I have. That is why even today I still use my transfer board for lots of manoeuvres where I could manage without one. I have to face facts, I am not getting any younger. I am a middle-aged woman and yes I am fit and healthy, but I am not in my twenties. My body is now just teetering on the edge of decline. I also feel my accident and injuries have aged me slightly. It is a fact that the strain a spinal injury has on the body also knocks about fifteen years off your life expectancy. I really need to preserve all I have to see me through the years when I am older.

March 2nd

I've had a really great day today, although I've actually been a bit naughty. I had some friends round, one of whom has an absolutely beautiful golden retriever called Tom. We took Tom to the Co-op with us and felt bad about leaving him outside. I suggested we took him in to 'help' me. He walked really nicely by my chair and was so well behaved. After about fifteen minutes we were approached by a supervisor. He and two security men had been watching us from upstairs and just wanted to check that Tom was a disability dog. I said he was in training and getting used to the chair but couldn't pick things up yet. In a way he was, training had begun as soon as we had walked into the Co-op. The supervisor was quite happy and went about his way. I have to say it felt really comforting having Tom by my side and a disability dog is a definite must in my eyes.

March 3rd

I have had a wonderful day! I had my first wee in public, well a disabled toilet, which now means I'm not tied to rushing home but can stay out ALL day! I also went out to one of my old haunts – Pizza Express in Arundel – and I had the warmest welcome ever. Everyone said I looked amazing and came and had a chat and we had the best service and best food. I finished the night off with a cup of tea in my standing frame. It is the best feeling standing after a meal. Perfect end to an absolutely perfect day!

> *Conquering the weeing in public was such an important achievement. I can't stand, excuse the pun, the thought of being restricted to times and where I can go. The need for independence is the fuel that drives me forward to achieve as much as I can. I hate being dictated to by my disability to what I can and can't do and I guess this is a good attitude to have. It makes me sad to think, though, how many people with disabilities don't go out because they don't think they can.*

March 4th

People say animals are intuitive and this cat really, really is. He was a complete loner and a very elusive cat before I came home from hospital, yet now it's like he is my protector. When I come downstairs on my chairlift he follows a step behind the whole way and then jumps onto my wheelchair at the bottom. He doesn't move until I've practically transferred on top of him and then he moves on to my lap. Here

he will stay for ages while I wheel around going about my business. When I stand in my frame again he jumps on my chair as if preventing anyone else from using it. He also curls up with me when I sleep if he is about. We have become very close, but I do have to watch out for pick marks from his claws in my knees as of course I can't feel them!

March 5th

My lovely big girl is working tomorrow so she made me a special 'Hello Kitty' Mother's Day breakfast. Mother's Day this year is going to be a very poignant and special one for me. My children are the key motivation factors that have kept me going and kept me strong; being a mum is the best thing in the world for me and I cherish that with all my heart!

16.07

Just back indoors from having the best fun! A trip to the Co-op turned into a skateboard wheelchair rally, zooming round the block racing each other without a care in the world. I can't imagine what people must have thought seeing us both, a middle-aged woman in a wheelchair and a young lad on a skateboard hurtling down the road – but who cares when you are having that much fun!

March 6th

A very happy Mothering Sunday. Such a very, very special day today! I have been looking through Joseph's baby book as today I was able to enter the most significant entry. His birthday. It's so lovely for me to be able to celebrate his birthday with him at home. I missed two of my children's birthdays, including Meg's eighteenth being in hospital. For me the greatest pleasure and gift I have in life is being a mum. I nearly had that

gift taken away a few months ago. I am so grateful I am here today to be able to share more precious moments with the ones I love.

> *So many lovely things have happened to me since my accident. I certainly believe it was meant to be. Only once in the twelve years that Joseph has been alive has Mother's Day fallen on his birthday. It seems ironic it happens after I have a serious accident and spend two of my children's birthdays in hospital. It does maybe sound cheesy, and I know I keep saying it, but I am such a lucky lady and have so much to be grateful for.*

March 7th

I had such a fantastic Mother's Day with my children yesterday but the highlight of my day was Jacob's amazing portrait of me! I think he captured me perfectly with my big smile, although I think a pair of arms may have been helpful. It made me laugh so much. It made us all laugh. The Mona Lisa has nothing on me! Oh, and for those who don't know, Jacob is my sixteen-year-old!

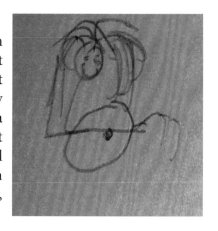

March 9th

Good morning. This may seem like a daft thing to say but one of my favourite pleasures every day is someone opening the curtains for me as I can't reach them any more. It's such a poignant event for me. I try and anticipate what the weather is going to be before they are opened. I get quite excited at the prospect of a brand new day and the sky, whatever colour, is like a blank page of paper for me to fill up. It just makes me feel so positive that every day I am given the chance to start afresh. If I have had a bit of a crap day the day before where things may have not gone to plan, I now have the opportunity for a good one. I'm going to fill my page with good, happy things today.

19.09

A friend was trying to put my chair in the back of her car but the car parked next to her was too close so she couldn't get the driver's door open properly! 'Don't worry,' I piped up, 'I'll get out and you can put the chair in my side.' Doh! I would have had fun trying, that's for sure.

March 11th

This picture of my first visit to West Dean gardens doesn't quite do it justice. Today was one of those days where words can't quite describe how content you feel, but the peace and tranquillity in the sunshine said it all.

March 12th

It's been a while since this little number has been out of the wardrobe but today's the day. I'm participating in the Bognor parkrun. Last time I ran wearing this vest, it was the summer. A lot has happened since then and it will be my first 'running' event in my chair. I'm feeling pretty nervous but I can't wait to meet up with my running buddies who are helping this morning.

12.18

Overwhelmed by the massive welcome and support at Bognor parkrun today. A touching mention from Keith too. My lovely friends who accompanied me on my way round had to put up with my constant chatter and noise, but when it started to hurt a bit they were such a great distraction. Lots of cake at the end as well. I have a feeling I might be back again. I felt AWESOME!

Being back amongst all my running friends felt amazing. Everyone was so pleased to see me. I guess it must also be so hard for them seeing me in a wheelchair. I know from being a runner how you feel when you can't run for some reason or other. It is the worst feeling in the world. They all know that I will never run again. The point is that until something actually happens to you, you don't know exactly how you are going to feel. To be totally honest I don't miss my running like I thought I would as my life is so full in other ways. I do get strong pangs for it sometimes and it makes me so sad, but it is short-lived. I certainly felt nothing but fulfilment today. It was so good to be back.

My experience yesterday was a tiny insight into how amazing the real athletes in wheelchairs are and how tough they have it when they train. I only did a 5k and very slowly at that. When I finished, my arms and hands were like jelly. I couldn't just rest them like I would my legs, I had to carry on using them. I nearly couldn't hold my piece of cake and eat it, that would have been a total disaster! Arms are smaller and weaker limbs than our good old legs but now they do everything, while Bert and Ernie enjoy a long holiday! Even texting and using my fingers ached where I'd been gripping the wheels. I still had to use my arms though, and carry on with my transfers. The best rest I got was standing in my frame letting my arms just rest on the tray. The real athletes train every day and reach speeds on their handbikes with arm power I never even reached using my legs on my bike. Many train and race with torn muscles as they are not able to give their limbs the rest they need, but sheer determination drives them on. They then carry on with their normal lives continuing to use just one set of limbs. I will be watching the Rio Paralympics this year with a totally new understanding and respect.

Since the parkrun on Saturday, I had received a real wake-up call as to how long my body was going to take adjusting to the physical demands my new life was having on it. I thought I would come home from hospital and be whizzing around everywhere. I would be upping my miles in my chair ready for my marathon in October with Ben Smith and getting on with day-to-day tasks in my new body. This was not to be. Just three miles in my chair had absolutely wiped me out! I couldn't be trying to increase my distance in that and also transferring and moving around. The impact on my arms and upper body was massive and it really did come as a shock to me how hard it was just moving around on a daily basis in my chair. I was learning everything took time and I was just going to have to be patient. This was turning out to be the biggest lesson in patience I had ever had.

March 14th

Another important goal achieved today. Mirrors were put up in the house at midget height. I have on several occasions left the house without checking myself in the mirror first. This has knocked my confidence a little as not only am I in a wheelchair but I could quite possibly look awful too. Until now I have only had a little compact mirror but today all that changed. It's just simple things that make you feel normal and good about yourself. If I go out looking awful now, I have no excuse!

March 16th

'What is this life if, full of care, we have no time to stand and stare' – a nurse at Stoke told me one thing I'd gain from my injury was time, and that I would really appreciate it. She was so right, I made sure I took that time today. I sat for twenty minutes in the conservatory in the late-evening sun with my cat on my lap. I've had a tough old day today, as we all do from time to time, and that twenty minutes was the best ever.

Restriction in movement around the house was very, very frustrating. Combined with the chronic pain, lack of independence, inability to just go out whenever and wherever I pleased, and being at home alone, it really got to me some days, as it would anyone. My whole world had been flipped upside down. Getting in the conservatory since my accident was impossible on my own. This really upset me as it was my little sun trap. When I was able-bodied I would love just sitting out there on a cold sunny winter's day with the sun streaming through the windows warm on my face. Rosie would sit on the sofa next to me and we would be happy as anything just sat there together. I no longer had Rosie and I couldn't sit in the sun. The step stopping me from getting out was no problem as an able-bodied person. I used to step over it without giving it a thought. Now it might as well have been Mount Everest in my wheelchair, it was impossible to wheel over. To be helped out there later in the day by a family member to catch the last rays of sun was worth waiting for and I cherished every second of it. Silly, silly things like stepping over a step were really prominent in my mind as I realised just how much I had lost.

March 17th

What a GLORIOUS day. I had a trial on a handbike and managed to get the rep, who is also in a wheelchair, stuck on a muddy pathway with me. I was trying to get into the fields where I used to walk Rosie. We had to get an able-bodied person to help us out! I also had a gentle reminder today as to how lucky I am to be here. To be honest though, I think the same every day. I met a fellow dog walker who is coincidently friends with a paramedic who was at the scene of my accident. Apparently I was the talk of Worthing ambulance station for a good two weeks after the event. I am every paramedic's dream accident victim. They all train for

that really horrific, adrenaline rush, near fatal accident where they can put all their training into practice. Most often they don't get the chance. Thanks to me, two paramedics did. Lucky for me they were well trained too. Of course the best part of the day was my twenty-minute cuddle in the sun with my boy, the cat.

March 18th

I know I say it quite often and it must get boring, but I am truly blessed to have such amazing friends. This morning I was procrastinating about getting up. I've been spoilt by the Mediterranean temperatures in hospital and struggle getting up in the cold. Plus several cups of tea are always helpful and I'd only had one. A knock at the door signalled an impromptu visit from a friend. The heating and kettle were on in minutes. Another knock on the door and another surprise visit. This time a friend with biscuits and money raised for me in a run. We sat upstairs drinking tea and eating biscuits just merrily chatting. I felt so special. After they left, an arranged visit from another friend. We visited the chip shop and I made the chip shop owner's day. He had brought new ramps for his shop and I was able to try them out for him. We left him a happy man. We then sat in the park eating chips. The cold made the chips even more appetising and I enjoyed watching my warm breath hit the cold air, simple things. As long as I am continuously surrounded by my brilliant friends I don't think I could be happier. Oh, and I think all of my nearest and dearest know where my front door key is, too!

March 19th

When my accident occurred I was in the middle of training my fifth guide dog puppy, Fareham. As a result, we sadly had to say goodbye to her. She left the very next day to continue her training elsewhere. In just over an hour we are going to have a visit from her to say a proper goodbye as she is going to start the next stage of her training. I'm so excited, I can't wait, but I'm sure I'm going to cry too.

16.54

Very mixed feelings about this beautiful girl. It would be lovely to see her pass and become a guide dog, but very selfishly, oh how I want her to fail so that I could have her as my disability dog! Que sera sera.

March 20th

Pain is a funny old thing, especially neuropathic pain. Since I've been home my sensations have developed and changed. When I have a shower and hot water hits my left shoulder, I get really horrid sensations in my left foot. It is similar to when your hands are freezing cold and you plunge them into hot water. If you cut my left foot off though, which theoretically would cause real pain, I wouldn't feel it! When I used to run I always remember the saying that running is 1 per cent physical and 99 per cent mental when things got tough and it hurt! Since my accident I am more aware than ever of how true this is. Our brain affects so many physical feelings and controls so much. Also I realise how amazing and complex our nervous system is. I also chuckle when I remember my running friends telling me about running being 99 per cent mental and then adding, 'and you Mandy are just 100 per cent mental!'

March 21st

A friend posted a quote which I keep thinking about. Life isn't about arriving in our grave at the end with a gentle landing in a beautiful well-preserved body. We should skid in sideways on, having really enjoyed life. We should take a few risks and have a few adventures along the way. I think I will hit my grave head first and with a body half broken. When I do I want to be able to say I lived it to the full. I also hope, but can't guarantee, that I have a few more years left in which to live it even fuller.

March 22nd

Really excited as today my super-duper, all-singing, all-dancing watch arrived! I bought it with money raised from Bognor Regis Tone Zone running club who I ran with. I was unable to phone for help when I had my accident as my phone was thrown from my pocket.

Since my accident I have felt quite scared about falling out of my chair or getting into another predicament. With my new watch I can call for help if my phone is out of reach, which has given me real peace of mind. Money well spent I think. It even has a pedometer on it and Bert and Ernie amazingly managed 1,663 steps today, which is 0.8 of a mile! They must have snuck off and done that when I wasn't looking.

My super-duper watch. Since my accident I am more nervous about the prospect of being on my own. Having a watch that enables me to make a phone call even if my phone is out of reach gives me real peace of mind. The trauma of a bad accident affects people in many different ways. Some people blot it out completely, some people suffer from post-traumatic syndrome and some people, like me, seem to sail through it quite well. I am lucky because the accident hasn't traumatised me too much. I don't even get upset when I drive past the place on Bury Hill. It has just taught me to try and be a little more careful and maybe not to take as many big risks any more. I nearly lost my precious family and the most important thing to me is to make sure I never risk losing them again.

March 24th

Every morning when I wake up I look down at my legs and see them staring straight back at me, reminding me of all that I've lost. Simultaneously it just reinforces how immensely lucky I am for what I have. Easter holidays start tomorrow and I can't wait just to have quality time with my children. I treasure that more than anything.

March 25th

Today started early with a drive to Queen Elizabeth Country Park to meet the Queen Elizabeth Spring half and full marathon race director at 9.15am. I feel completely honoured and privileged to be starting both debut races next Sunday. Today I had a run-through of what was expected of me. I'm not fit or strong enough to take part in races yet. All my strength and energy goes into just living my day-to-day life. It's so much more demanding on my upper body than I ever imagined. Despite this I'm still desperate to be involved in racing in some way. Phil the director has given me a really great opportunity on Sunday. We finished off with breakfast in the sunshine. A brilliant productive start to the Easter Weekend.

March 27th

Having spent Christmas in hospital, celebrating Easter at home has been much more significant this year. The Easter Bunny struggled a bit as she wasn't able to hop about like she did last year. Some of the eggs on the Easter egg hunt were 'thrown' into hiding places rather than placed. I missed my Christmas tradition of making a Christmas cake so was determined to make my Easter cake. That also proved a bit of a challenge. The kitchen looked like a flour bomb had gone off in it and the cat got a covering as well. I've loved being home today so much, just enjoying simple but quality time with my family.

21.52

Ben Smith is one of the nicest people you could ever meet. I am really proud to have met and to have run a 5k with him. I feel so lucky to be able to call him my friend as he finds time with everything else he is doing to message me and find out how I am. Please take a few moments to read his story online. It will blow you away.

March 28th

There are many emotions a person goes through with a spinal injury. One of those is grief. I had a little cry last night. Bert and Ernie are little shits a lot of the time, they give me a lot of pain and make life twice as hard with their spasms. I bent over to check my skin on my legs and feet and I don't know why but I kissed them – and they smelt of me and I felt so sorry for them and burst into tears. They are actually still part of me but a lot of the time they don't feel like they are! On a happy note I went and bought Big Wig, my bunny, a new front-opening cage today so now I can get him out for a cuddle myself and not rely on others. I also sat outside in the sun and had a hot chocolate; hard to believe we had a storm last night as the sun was so warm today.

It is so bizarre how you can build up a relationship with part of your body. My legs used to be a working part connected to the rest of my body and working in harmony with it. When I was triathlon training my body worked like a finely tuned engine. Now it was like an old banger and my legs would quite often work against me and not with me. Some days they could just feel like useless lumps of meat dangling down in front of me and I would just want to chop them off. Then when I felt calmer, for example in the morning just waking up, I would look down at them and feel waves of guilt for hating them so much and then I would miss them.

March 29th

I received this picture yesterday from Amelia Worne. I feel it is always so important to remember that there is always a calm after a storm. Often a storm is needed to clear the air. There have been a few storms in our household since I've come home from hospital. It wouldn't be a normal household if there weren't. The good thing is, though, that everyone is comfortable to air their

opinions and say how they feel. Ultimately, after each storm the sun shines even brighter and stronger than before.

March 30th

Bit of a frustrating day today. It's hard in the holidays not driving as I can't just pop in the car and take the children out and do nice holiday things with them. I tried to sort out my assessment for trying out hand-controls which will be fitted in my new car, only to be told there is a TEN WEEK wait – ten more weeks with no driving. Not the end of the world but frustrating nonetheless. I decided to spend quality time with my two youngest at home, so we played a board game. We used Bert and Ernie as a table. This was going well until Ernie decided he'd had enough and kicked the board up in the air! This really made us all laugh and it made me realise it's all about making the best of what you've got and I am so rich – in fact far richer than many with what I have.

March 31st

As the saying goes – 'Everything happens for a reason.' The fact I have to wait six weeks for a driving assessment is no longer a problem. I received a phone call today saying there is a delay on my car. It should be ready in July! At least it's not further major surgery I'm waiting for and at least I have so many dear friends who have been ferrying me about. I have had a lovely day at home making chocolate fountains and cuddling guinea pigs in the sun. All good things come to those who wait.

April 2016

April 1st

Someone rummaging through my running gear this morning getting ready for a run. It's a beautiful day and I'd be going too if I could. It's nice to see my stuff still getting used and not just collecting dust. I've told Amelia to run well and love

her legs and not to take them for granted. I feel happy that she enjoys running and experiences the feelings I used to feel. I'd be telling stories, though, if I said it doesn't make my heart pull towards the door and want to go with her. Happy running to all those who go out today.

April 2nd

Today is the day that a lot of people remember and rejoice on the day you were born, especially me. Happy fourteenth birthday my Amelia Worne.

> *The realisation that your children are growing up so fast and the rejoicing in the fact that you are still here to share these special days with them.*

April 3rd

Today was a really special day. I turned up at my first race. The Queen Elizabeth half and full Spring marathons. I was going to be the race starter today. I still felt nervous, as I would if I were running, and excited too. I could also feel the same buzz in the air from all the runners preparing to race. It was so lovely to be with my all my running buddies again. It did feel strange blowing the horn and watching everyone run off! I made myself busy and helped marshal the marathon runners on to a second lap and directing the half-marathon runners to the finish. Three hours was enough for me though, sounds a bit corny but my back was hurting sitting in one place and I was getting cold. The race director was lovely and pushed me down the hill and to my surprise pushed me through the finishing tunnel and over the finish line. He then presented me with the first full marathon medal too, which was beautiful and I did well

up! I enjoyed today but it did make me realise more than ever that I can't wait to be out there racing again, earning my medals to fill up my new medal rack, which so rightly says 'anything is possible'.

> *It's funny how people who were walking during the race made an effort to run as they went past by me. I guess I am a strong visual reminder of how lucky they are to be able to do what they are doing. I gave lots of support and encouragement as they went past as I wanted to be able to make them feel positive and good about themselves if they were struggling. I remember how important those words and shouts of support were to me. It is easier to achieve our goals and challenges with the support of others. No man is an island, I'm a firm believer in that.*

April 4th
Sharing a Baileys with a touch of chocolate ice cream with my special eldest girl tonight.

> *Simple pleasures with special people make the warmest happy feelings.*

April 6th
Really lovely when you phone a friend to invite her over for coffee and she takes you into town for some all-important chocolate shopping.

April 7th
I've been looking forward to today all week, as with help I was able to take my two youngest on a holiday treat. We all had a fab time but it was so, so busy with children and parents rushing everywhere. You seem to get in everyone's way in a wheelchair. I really have to pay much more attention to what is going on around me as my reactions are much slower and more

cumbersome. When I walked I never walked in a straight line and I think I'm worse in a chair. I'm always trying to avoid the bad paving stones and uneven paths. I nearly wheeled into a man today so I immediately looked at him, apologised and smiled. He smiled back and said thank you and that he couldn't hear me because he wasn't wearing his hearing aid but he had lip-read my apology. As he passed me he squeezed my shoulder. I'm in a world now where I feel a bit more vulnerable and everything is a bit more daunting. I think that's what his squeeze meant as he understood how I was feeling, too!

Life is so different when your movements are compromised for some reason or another. I really feel like such a wide load and I hate feeling like I am in the way. I have to overcome this feeling. I am not a burden, I have as much right as anyone to be out and about. I am not in the way, I am a member of society and on the whole people are very accommodating to my situation. All the years I have spent moving aside or opening a door or waiting patiently behind a wheelchair, now I am that person in that chair. It's my turn to view it from the other side and boy what a view it is!

April 8th

Well who would have thought, from marathon runner and triathlete to knitter! I'm trying to find things to occupy me while my strength builds and I can train like I used to. They say knitting is therapeutic. Well today it most certainly wasn't. I'm knitting a jumper and had to undo the fourth row at least five times. The language was ripe and the ball and needles nearly went across the room umpteen times. I feel I'm getting somewhere now though, I'll probably finish it in time for winter 2020!

April 9th

I'm turning into Madame Dafarge, a French tricoteuse from *A Tale of Two Cities*. Women used to sit and knit at the guillotine during the

French Revolution. I haven't witnessed any beheadings yet, although a disagreement between two teenagers came close! I'm absolutely loving it.

April 10th

Bags all packed and feeling excited. Tomorrow I'm going back up to Stoke Mandeville for the Interspinal Games. It will be fab to catch up with some of my friends and try out a load of new sports. I'll leave the knitting behind as I have a feeling I'll be too busy to do any.

Oh my, how nervous do I feel. Going back to Stoke Mandeville without the safety blanket of my family and not as a patient but as someone who is meant to be independent. What are the showers and toilets going to be like? Will the beds have proper pressure-relief mattresses? How will I unpack all my stuff and put it all away? So many questions and uncertainties are running through my head. It's my biggest challenge to date but I know I will deal with it in my own stride and come out the other side a stronger and better person for having done so.

April 11th

I've arrived! I've learnt my first important lesson: don't take Bert and Ernie to the loo when you are all hyped up and excited at seeing everyone again. They spasmed and went rigid on the toilet and I had to wait ages for them to calm down before I could get back on my chair. I thought I was going to be there all night!

Meeting up with my hospital buddies again was such a lovely feeling but this was counterbalanced by one of unsettlement. The accommodation we had for the spinal games was simply not overly wheelchair friendly, surprisingly enough, and it came as a shock to everyone. I had such a wobbly feeling in my tummy. How on earth would I cope for three days here without the accessibility we were all expecting? I just sat on my bed wondering what I was going to do. It was at this point that I noticed one of my friends sitting on her bed sobbing her heart out. She was in a much worse state about the situation than me. Instantly I forgot about my worries and wanted to reassure her that everything would be fine. I told her we were close to the hospital and could go up and use the facilities there, as I was sure we would be allowed to. I gave her a big hug. In my efforts to reassure her that it would be fine, I had in turn reassured myself. I wasn't alone and we would all get through this by helping and supporting each other.

April 12th

Having such an amazing but such a surreal time. I've been participating in sports all day. I met the lady who owns this pink wheelchair. She won the Paris Marathon a couple of weeks ago. I was about to have a turn, but the heavens opened and we had a massive thunderstorm. I went up to the hospital to visit a few friends, some of whom are still very poorly. I had a sudden overwhelming realisation of how lucky I truly am. I was pretty poorly not so long ago lying in one of those beds and here I am competing in so many amazing sports, so healthy and alive and so

much stronger than before. I rowed again for the first time in months and surprised myself completely by beating my old 30-second dash time by 10 seconds and actually being the fastest female, too.

April 14th

The spinal injured world is an amazing world to be in. I'm coming out of my comfort zone so, so many times. I took part in the swimming competition. I never enjoyed the swim on my triathlons and a swim race without leg use was a really daunting experience. I've not been in a swimming pool yet and getting down onto the edge of the pool and sliding into the water 'gracefully' in front of loads of people was really hard. The water was really cold, so I had to swim with Bert and Ernie in a complete state of shock as they protested to this fact and they locked rigid. I was in a race with two girls with quite a bit more experience than me, but I did it. I came third out of three and I even managed to drag myself out afterwards on my own. I've conquered my apprehension of going to the public pool now and can't wait to go again when I get home.

Times and personal bests are no longer a priority now. Just getting out there and taking part is the most important thing. My whole view of competing has totally changed. I no longer beat myself up if I don't think I was fast enough or as good as someone else. I actually feel proud of myself for just being brave enough to do it. Theoretically we should all just be proud of our achievements as long as we know we have given everything we have and tried our hardest, but human nature is hard and makes us always feel we should have done more. My accident has allowed me to adopt a different attitude and I prefer the one I now have. Just do your best and be happy with your achievements. Life is too short to beat yourself up all the time. Just enjoy it even if you come last like I did.

April 15th

Just home from one of the most amazing weeks in my life. I feel completely honoured and privileged to have been chosen to take part in such a significant event. It wasn't all about the winning or competing, it was about the overall experience that will help me through life in my chair. I've learnt so many more wheelchair skills and gained so much more confidence. I met some very special and humbling people who really made me realise more than ever just how lucky I am. To make the week complete though, the Stoke Mandeville team were the overall winners of the Interspinal Games of 2016, coming first out of sixteen teams. I will treasure this week in my heart for always.

April 16th

A well-earned hot chocolate as today I helped direct my first ever park run. I was told I was a natural with the pre-run speech – I can't think why? Looking forward to tomorrow as I'm going to support a lot of my friends running the Brighton Marathon. I can honestly say, hand on heart, that I don't feel sad that I can't do it. I've run four marathons in my time including London, all with very different experiences. I am very lucky to have been able to do that and my week away showed me I can have just as many happy experiences in my chair. I will have my loudest voice at the ready and cowbells jingling to encourage all my running buddies home.

April 17th

What a fantastic day with a lovely friend. There is definitely more satisfaction and happiness to be had from supporting others in obtaining their goals than achieving your own, and a lot less pressure too. So pleased to have seen so many friendly faces and cheer them on and absolutely blown away to see Ben 401 marathon runner. So much so that I fell out of my chair!

I learnt today that it is possible to go out for the whole day in my wheelchair and not worry about toilet stops. I have been anxious about not being able to find a loo if I go to places I am not familiar with, but I buried that fear today. I have to be a little more organised and plan ahead a bit more but being in a wheelchair doesn't and shouldn't stop you from doing what you want to do.

April 18th

Back to normality today and struggling with putting wet washing on airers and boring housework. Last week seems like a dream; well the swim was a nightmare but I am hoping to go again soon and face my demons. I hope any marathon runners today aren't hurting too much. I bet they would love to borrow my chairlift for the stairs!

I know I joke a lot about running a marathon and how sore, achy runners would benefit from my chairlift, as dealing with the stairs hurts their legs so much. I remember feeling exactly the same myself. I am only human though, and when you see it posted everywhere on Facebook, although I make light of it, there are times I think how lucky these people are that at least they can still feel their legs. Even the most positive people have to sometimes have down times and sad feelings and that includes me.

April 19th

Felt a bit flat this morning after a really fantastic week and weekend. I have so much independence and freedom back at Stoke. At home there are still so many restrictions and frustrations. A nice breakfast with a lovely marathon running friend soon lifted my mood. I offered her the use of my chairlift for the stairs but she bravely declined! I also miss the companionship of a dog, especially as the weather is improving. Another dear friend took me to visit the bluebells and she let me borrow her dog. Such a beautiful walk and the smell was divine. I was even brave enough to race down a hill with my four-legged friend in hot pursuit. Feeling confident in my chair, when I got home I practised some backwheel balancing with anti-tips on the highest setting. They didn't work and I found myself in a daze flat on my back. The thought of this has petrified me but guess what – it's not as bad as you think. Like most things in life it's the thought that's often worse than the actual thing itself.

April 19th is an example of a day where I started off feeling a bit flat and not so positive. Invariably there are not many days that start off like this that don't improve as the day progresses. This is because I hate feeling down for too long and always strive to find something positive to do. I think there are some people who go through life only happy if they have something to moan about, but I'm not one of these people. I love life and I love laughing and smiling and feeling happy. To me that is what life should be about. Face the challenges, overcome them and try and come out smiling the other side.

April 20th

Had a really brilliant day today. Had my first hydro session since Stoke. It was so beneficial. My legs, hips and lower back are really tight and quite sore where I don't get to move around as much as I did. It's also the reason why Bert and Ernie spasm – it's because they hurt. Hydro was amazing I had two physios and they spent well over an hour loosening everything. I did a lot of core work strengthening as well and stood for the first time with help in water. I'm being used as a guinea pig for a case study, so I get extra hydro sessions too. As always I didn't want to get out of the shower as I still really appreciate them. I also decided to make a really nice salad for tea as hospital salads are so bland and now I can choose exactly what I eat and don't have to stick to a hospital menu.

April 21st

I awoke this morning to see the post, which I have just shared. I think it is so heartless for anyone to steal a handbike from someone in a wheelchair, as now being in one myself I realise just what significance a handbike really has. It's our freedom, our escapism, our release from the confinements of one space and a place where we can feel normal and also a place where we feel strong and enpowered. Please share the post too as this bike means everything to my friend and I really hope we get it back to him.

18.14

For the first time today I've seen physically how far I've come since August and how broken my body was. I am absolutely chuffed and amazed with the results. It's been a bit of a tough physical journey these past months but my hard work and all the pain has really paid off. I really feel like at long last my fitness is returning!

April 22nd

My friend's bike is still missing but at least it has made the news. A big thank you to those who shared it's disappearance, too.

April 23rd

Not only did Gary save my life but he volunteers at a sailing club for people with disabilities and guess who got to have a go at sailing today. I spent the best time ever with Amelia and Kerry just messing about in boats. I thank

God every day for being so lucky to still be here and on days like today I cherish that more than ever.

> *It felt quite surreal sitting peacefully bobbing along in a boat with Gary. We were sharing a relatively normal pleasant experience together. It was a complete contrast to the time we had shared waiting for the ambulance. I am sure that was a very stressful experience for Gary, as well as it being a very scary experience for me. It was also very bizarre how life had thrown us together. I don't think many friendships start off the way ours did. At that moment I just felt so content. It was a moment I will always remember.*

April 24th

Two years ago I ran the London Marathon. It was a total disaster. Hedley, my guide dog puppy, had died the day before of cancer, I started in the wrong pen, my Garmin watch broke and I ran over 27 miles in 4.02 and I so wanted to finish in sub 4! I've been watching today's London Marathon and haven't stopped crying. I've watched elite men and women runners and the wheelchair racers too, and can relate this year to both types of athletes. I saw my friend Ben Smith interviewed on his 401 marathon quest and who would have ever thought a local astronaut, Tim Peake who comes from Chichester, would start the race running it himself from space! Today the millionth runner to run the London Marathon will cross the line. I really feel so emotional and proud to have been one of those million runners. I think whether you run or don't run, are able-bodied or not, today is truly a memorable day in English history.

> *I think I cried today partly because I missed my legs. I was grieving for something that I had lost. I had lots of memories doing great things as an able-bodied person, and the London Marathon was one of those things.*

It was also a time that I had lost something else very dear to me. I had lost Hedley the guide dog puppy very suddenly to a rare form of blood cancer. My new life was proving to be fulfilling, but even so, when you lose something precious be it a loved one or in my case my legs, although you move on you never forget the thing you have lost and sometimes you are allowed days where you still really miss it or them.

April 25th

Back in hospital I ran/wheeled a 5k with Ben Smith who was attempting to run 401 marathons. We bundled along together so nicely I could have done at least half a marathon if not more. I was having such a great time. He made me feel on top of the world. That evening Ben visited me in my hospital bed with framed photos of our time together and ever since he has kept in touch to see how I'm doing. He actually cares wholeheartedly about his cause and the people he meets. His sporting achievement is astounding and he deserves every piece of recognition he gets.

16.21

This week marks three months since I left Stoke Mandeville hospital. Ever since that day I have had flowers on my table and chocolate or cake in my cupboard. It's quite amazing I'm not the size of a house! I have not spent one single day alone. I've either had friends popping round or friends taking me out! I've even had a lot of money raised to help me buy things to give me my confidence and freedom back again. I am completetly surrounded by such lovely, beautiful people and nothing can ever compare to good friendships. They are to be treasured and have been the main incentive for my progress and rehabilitation. I really want to thank everyone so much. I am truly blessed.

April 26th

Every morning a lot of us wake up, and the first thing we think of is the worry we went to bed with or what grotty task we may have to do that day. Mornings can be a little difficult. I wake up forgetting for an instant I can't walk and then it suddenly dawns on me that I can't! I fight with Bert and Ernie and struggle to sit up in bed and drink a very much needed cup of tea whilst looking out the window. I reflect on all the lovely things I have in my life including my hands to hold my teacup. I am so lucky

I don't have to wait until someone helps me drink it. I also think about all the good things that I have to look forward to. Mornings can be crap whatever, but like anything, you can turn it on it's head and make it better. Wishing everyone a really happy Tuesday morning and I hope if you are struggling you can flip it on its head, too.

April 28th

A three-month MOT at Stoke Mandeville and I couldn't not say hello to my friend Mr Poppa. All is good, I'm doing grand and even got to see my new piece of metal work I had done in December. David Guetta's song 'Titanium' certainly has a new meaning to me these days!

April 29th

I awoke this morning to find my beanie owl warmer I'd used the night before on my back stuck to my backside! Luckily there were no damaging marks. My bottom always gets more looks in the mirror these days than my face! I had a lovely lunch too in a beautiful little café with a lovely lady. We had a blustery walk along the seafront afterwards, so it was nice to come home and have a hot bath. For the first few months baths have been a real disaster but I have really got them down to a fine art now and I cherish them. I still almost cry with pleasure and happiness when I sink back beneath the warm bubbles for the first time. It's just one of the nicest experiences you can have for cold aching muscles and bones, I remember the same feeling well after a long, cold and wet Sunday-morning run!

April 30th

Well, I finally got to try out a proper racing chair and spent a happy time racing up and down the track! It felt very different than I expected it to, much better in fact, and it really did feel lovely with the sun and wind in my face pootling along without a care in the world!

I really thought that lying with my knees scrunched up underneath me would be a lot more painful. It wasn't too bad at all but I didn't get the feeling that it was something that I would like to pursue. I had all these ideas in hospital of what I was going to do, but now that I was out these ideas weren't really panning out. I was making decisions and plans from a hospital bed without a clue what wheelchair life was really like. Now I was actually living the life in a wheelchair, I realised just how different things actually were. I was adamant on the day of the accident that I would race my friends in my pink racing chair, yet I just didn't get a buzz like I thought I would. I also found it quite hard work on my back but at least I had tried it and had a go. It was still early days. I had only been home from hospital for a few months so maybe it was something I would try again at a later date. I had my whole life ahead of me and there was no need to rush.

May 2016

May 2nd

Happy Bank Holiday despite the weather! Due to the fact it's a bit grotty today, I am even more grateful that with the help of Amelia I managed to get out in the garden yesterday. It was the first time in almost six months. It's been a little while but I have another spinal injury fact to share. I had a blood test up at Stoke on Thursday to check my vitamin D levels. Apparently people with spinal damage are prone to vitamin D deficiency. This is because where we no longer stand our bones lose density and become very weak. This can lead to them breaking very easily. The sun is the best form of vitamin D, so I have more excuse now than ever to soak up its rays when we are lucky enough to see it.

May 3rd

A beautiful sunny morning and I'm going on a road trip adventure to Liverpool. I'm off to collect my handbike attachment for my chair. I'm really excited as it will make life so much easier and give me even more independence – and that's what it's all about!

18.11

I've got my bike attachment and do you know what – it's absolutely brilliant and I can see it being worth every penny to me! Life is great and it just keeps getting better and better.

Since having my accident I am starting to realise just how expensive wheelchair accessories and equipment are, and also how far you have to travel to get them as there are not many places in the country that do them. Also, the demand for them is high so people can basically charge what they want. It's a real shame as many miss out because they just can't afford them. I thought cycling was expensive but it is nothing compared to the cost of the wheels I need now. I've been so fortunate with good friends supporting me and helping raise money for the things I need to give me my independence back again.

May 4th

ANOTHER beautiful sunny day and I've entered the wheelchair ballot for the London Marathon! Everything including Bert and Ernie are crossed that I get in.

May 5th

First time behind the wheel thanks to my fab friend Paul Helyer who is a wheelie like me! He let me drive his hand-controlled car, which is what I should hopefully soon have. What a TOTALLY AMAZING feeling to be driving again. What is so encouraging is that being with Paul, I see how independent I can become. He makes things look so simple and nothing is impossible. I always leave his company feeling totally empowered and capable of doing anything! No mountain is too high.

May 6th

This time last year I had just found my love for barefoot running. Post-marathon toes had made my trainers too uncomfortable to wear but I was still desperate to run. Our feet are amazing things, although a lot of us hate them. Here are some amazing foot facts:

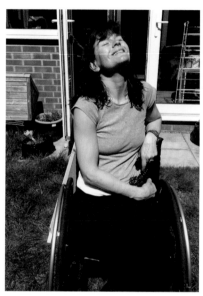

1) When running your toes effectively increase in length allowing you to run even faster.

2) A third of all the bones in the body are located in our feet. There are 26 of them, and each foot also has 33 joints, 19 muscles, 10 tendons and 107 ligaments.

3) When walking, each time your heel lifts off the ground it forces the toes to carry one half of your body weight.

4) During an average day of walking, the total forces on your feet can total hundreds of tons, equivalent to an average of a fully loaded cement truck.

5) Researchers have concluded that people had healthier feet and posture before the invention of shoes. The Zulu, who often go barefoot, have the healthiest feet of modern humans.

6) Butterflies taste with their feet, gannets incubate eggs under their webbed feet, and elephants use their feet to hear – they pick up vibrations of the earth through their soles.

7) The average person will walk around 115,000 miles in a lifetime, that's more than four times around the earth!

So even if you are a foot hater, love your feet today and thank them for the amazing job that they do.

I do feel quite sad about my feet. I used to actually quite like mine. As I started barefoot running I noticed how they became more muscular. Inside shoes and trainers our feet are supported so the muscles don't develop much. Barefoot running meant the muscles got used so much more. Now in the morning they just look so skinny and scrawny and at the end of the day they look fat and swollen. Glands in my legs are no longer able to disperse fluid around my body. At least they are not all purple and blotchy with poor circulation and I think I will still be able to wear flip-flops when the summer comes.

May 7th

I took part in my second parkrun today as Amanda 'Wheeler' with my new bike attachment. Managed to knock fourteen minutes off my last parkrun time, which shows how the new bike is much more efficient. I miss my legs and feet today, though. It's weird sitting in the garden in shorts with the sun shining on you and not feeling the warmth on your legs. It's also strange not being able to feel the grass beneath my feet. I still thank my lucky stars for all I have. I am so blessed in many ways, but at the same time though, I am still coming to terms with what I have lost.

> *I loved the parkrun but it is funny. When I finish I just want to get up and run. Using my arms doesn't give me an all-over body workout like running used to. I think I will always miss that but I have friends who can't even use a handbike so I am very lucky for what I still have.*

May 8th

Feeling very brave today. The sun is shining and it's beautiful. I'm taking Bert and Ernie out uncovered and on show to the world for the first time since my accident. Wearing flip-flops is an interesting experience too. I can't grip them with my toes and they've fallen off a couple of times. For the first year in quite a few though, I have no marathon toes, so there's no way I'm covering them in shoes!

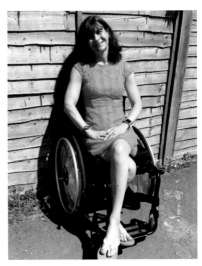

May 9th

I am such a very lucky lady and have so many amazing and generous friends. So many have gone out of their way to help raise much-needed funds for me and I am forever grateful for this. It also got me thinking. I decided today it was about time I got off my lazy backside and started helping too. Today marks the nine-month anniversary of my accident. With the initial idea implanted in my brain by Kerry Stafford, I have decided to mark my year anniversary with something truly memorable! Megan Worne, Kerry and I will be jumping out of an aeroplane a mile and a half up in the air and parachuting back down to the ground at about 120mph. It beats the heck out of hitting a metal post at 50mph, that's for sure! Hopefully our efforts may raise a bit of money for the wet room that I so desperately need. A 'just giving page' will follow and at the moment I am sitting here thinking what on earth have I done? But hey, you only live once!

> *I had often thought about doing a skydive but it is one of those things that you just think about but don't bother to actually do anything about. My accident made me realise that you only get one shot at this life and I felt I had been given a second chance. Therefore I was going to make sure I didn't waste it. I felt that a skydive was a really good way to really embrace life. A total contrast to the day a year earlier when I lay in bushes unable to move and totally broken. Instead I would fly through the air like a bird totally free.*

May 10th

I absolutely LOVE my hydro sessions! We discovered that I have a bit more movement today. My hip flexors work and I think they engage with my quads a little too. All positive stuff. I've had such a brilliant day; some days I just feel a real sense of peace and real contentment and today is one of them. I am so much more in tune with myself since my accident; maybe it's my age or maybe I have more time for reflection and appreciation. I'm not sure what the specific reason is, but today has been a really special day – it might just have been the simple fact that I had TWO straws in my drink!

May 11th

Well, I've taken the plunge. After a really lovely email from the race director of 'The Midsummer 5 Mile Race' giving me the go ahead and making me feel very welcome, I have entered my first race! I'm back out there again with a focus and something to train for. It's less than a year since I could even get out of bed and less than six months since my really big bout of surgery. Today I really feel I have taken a massive step forward, so to speak. Bert and Ernie are tapping on my footplate and I'm sure it's because they can sense how much I'm buzzing with excitement!

May 12th

Today was a day filled with beautiful fur babies. I had cuddles this morning with Xenia-Scarlet and a lovely catch-up with Kari. Then furry cuddles this afternoon with Honey, a beautiful yellow lab puppy. I had tea and egg mayonnaise sandwiches in the garden with Bex in the sunshine. We sat and watched Honey try and eat every flower or plant in sight. I did a bit more sitting than Bex as she ran round after Honey! Finally, on the way home we had to let Mrs Duck cross the road with her babies. There are beautiful new green leaves on the trees and summer is just starting. New life everywhere and I'm really loving my new life too.

May 13th

I feel like I've crammed the most amazing week's summer holiday into one day. Starting with a lovely lunch at the Lobster Pot, and then a wheel along the prom, a whole six-MILE wheel too! We met and chatted to people along the whole way. I felt really proud and happy as I got so many lovely compliments about my BIKE. NOT my wheelchair but my amazing BIKE! THAT really made me so happy. Sparky the dog liked my bike so much he decided to join me. The highlight of the day had to be wheeling along the sand and in the sea. I pondered many a night in hospital how I was going to get on to the beach and today I did. I felt such a sense of freedom and achievement, the best feeling ever. To have all these visions and hopes and be able to conquer them makes you feel invincible. Who needs legs when you have all this!

16.10

Wheeling along the sand was exhilarating but I couldn't stop as my wheels sunk.

I met a man with an amazing dog today, too. A little Jack Russell called Sparky who was quite happy to jump up and sit on my lap. He was absolutely adorable and I felt I wanted a dog just like him. I can't believe I am considering a lap dog. To me a dog has to be a substantial size to be called a dog. Otherwise it is just a rat and a Jack Russell too. I hate them as they are renowned for being snappy and mean. No one in my family will be impressed either, but we will see. I am not ready for a dog yet but I wonder that when I am, what I will actually get.

May 14th

I've overdone things today. I've discovered for me personally my body isn't as forgiving if I overdo things compared to when I was able-bodied. Firstly, if I strain my arms and shoulders, I can't sit with them 'up' like you do with your legs if you've pushed them a bit hard. Secondly, I have a lot more spasms as my body is protesting about what I've done. The spasms aren't just in my legs. Quite often they are in my tummy and they really hurt. The neuropathic pain is a lot worse as well. When I transfer my legs, rather than move freely, they resist and tighten and it's like lugging two big tree stumps around. Thing is, if I don't push myself how am I going to get stronger? We all ache and feel niggles and pain when we push a bit hard if we train. I think, though, that it makes us appreciate the good results more as it makes all the hardships and pain worthwhile. I must also remember, however, that a rest day is as good as a training day, so tomorrow I'll try and take it a bit easier.

May 15th

I slept like a baby last night and think maybe I was still dreaming this morning. What an unbelievable, magical, totally overwhelming time at the Bognor Regis 10k. So proud to see so many friendly faces from the running club and to be able to start them off in their race. It took 7 minutes to cheer all 1,400 runners past and such a joy to cheer them over the finish. I got lots of hot sweaty hugs too. I even got invited to give out the prizes with the Mayor of Bognor. I had a lovely

chat with James Baker and he even managed to lift me off the stage after the awards, despite the fact he had just run his 10k and come in second place! Days like today need saving in bottles so I can open them up again sometime as I still can't believe it's true. Thank you to all those responsible for arranging such a special day!

> *I sometimes feel I get treated like royalty! I am so lucky that people go out of their way to make things happen for me. It is a really lovely feeling and I cherish it so much. Even James Baker, who is a local running hero, made me feel like the hero at parkrun. How ironic is that!*

May 16th

Thinking about Meg and Jacob sitting exams today. I'm sure all their hard work will pay off and I'm so proud of them both.

21.08

I am really enjoying the freedom and liberty I have gained with my handbike. My next challenge is for me to gain my independence within my own home. For this reason, my daughter Megan Worne, my close friend Kerry Stafford and myself will be jumping out of a plane to raise money to build a wet room. I really hope you will continue with your great support on my journey, to help me in my efforts to remove the restrictions I face at home on a day-to-day basis.

May 17th

Standing in my frame is so beneficial but can be quite tedious. It is also sadly something that doesn't come natural to my body any more and can be uncomfortable and hard work. I've mentioned before that animals are intuitive, and my cat is unbelievable. He started off this evening sitting on my chair behind me. He cautiously ventured up onto my frame with me. Finally he tried to catch a fly. When I get down I have to be careful I don't sit on him if he is back on my chair. He is such a comfort to me in so many ways as I'm sure so many animals are to many. He certainly helps the time pass quickly with his antics. Life would be pretty dull without our four-legged friends.

May 18th

I had a really emotional afternoon today. With my lovely friend Lisa

Robinson, we drove to the Arun Leisure Centre. Many a time I have run from the there to the beach huts and back. A four-mile run. I used to run this way with Bognor Regis Tone Zone Runners. None of them were there, though. Club nights are Tuesday and Thursday. This was my first PROPER training run since my accident, and I almost cried as I came up the last little hill just before you get to the Leisure Centre. In my head I could see all my old running friends stretching after their runs, and I really felt like I was coming home, like I'd never been away! Maybe soon I'll venture back on a proper club night.

May 19th

I had four children at school in Arundel for thirteen years and never visited the Castle gardens. Well, today I did and they were breathtakingly beautiful and even magical and mystical in places. Like Alice in Wonderland where she visits the caterpillar. Time stood still for about an hour and all worries, cares and problems floated away. If you haven't ever been it's worth a visit. I'm so grateful I got the chance today. Thank you Amanda.

May 20th

An evening spent catching up with some lovely people at the Tone Zone Running awards. I received a very special welcome too. For some people it's the first time they've seen me in my chair and quite a few aren't on Facebook so haven't seen my progress. Lots of mixed reactions and mixed emotions but so special to catch up with the friends I've spent many happy hours running with.

I did find that it was very hard for some people at the Tone Zone presentation night to know what to say to me. I think that where they are all runners, it doesn't bear thinking about how awful it must feel to never be able to run again. A few told me not to give up hope and that they were sure I would run again someday. I tried to convince them that actually I was really happy with my new life and that it was highly unlikely that I would walk again. I have to accept, though, that people will not always see my spinal injury from my perspective and that also it is very hard to understand how you would feel about something until it happens to you. I post all the amazing things that are happening to me and I am sure people must see how much I am loving life. Of course there are hard days and sometimes just a little thing will trigger off a wave of emotions that I don't even expect, but that is all part of the grieving process. You can deal with the big things like not being able to walk, but not being able to reach the biscuits in the cupboard will be catastrophic! I have my difficult days like everyone, but hand on heart, my life is ultimately better now than it has ever been and I truly wouldn't change it for the world.

May 22nd

Well, sooner than I anticipated, first race booked in July, but this one has an amazing bit of bling so I thought I'd give it a go with fellow Tone Zone buddies Lisa Robinson and Helena. I'm feeling so nervous but excited!

15.24

It's hard to put into words how it felt being part of the racing circle again today. A small but tough 5k as far as I'm concerned, using my arms which are now my new legs, and boy did it hurt! Different surfaces including water, a few little inclines, and thick wet grass which was the real killer. A small grassy incline to the finish was the toughest as my big front wheel couldn't grip in the wet and the extra pressure of people cheering. At the line I burst into tears and sobbed. My first race in less than a year since almost killing myself and it was the best feeling ever!

May 23rd

Good morning, happy Monday! I've woken up, still smiling a massive smile after yesterday. I found a photo on the Second Wind running page that I think sums up exactly how I felt at the finish line. I'm feeling so lucky to be able to race again!

May 24th

Before my accident it's fair to say I had a pretty active life. I was swimming, cycling and running three times a week in training for a half Ironman. I was training Fareham my guide dog puppy and running round looking after my four amazing children. I hardly EVER sat down. Bert and Ernie (my legs) remember the life pre-accident and every morning they remind me how much they want to stand up and stretch. I have no control of them with my brain, but messages from my spinal cord still reach them willing them to walk. We argue every morning as I try and make them sit in my chair and they resist and lock dead straight. They tell me how much they want to stand. It's now 10am and I'm just downstairs having argued with them since 8.30am. They still aren't overly happy being forced into a wheelchair and I do actually feel guilty that my brain can't allow them to do what they want to do more than anything else in the world, which is walk. The sun is shining so I will pamper them with its rays and take them to hydro. I will also stand in my frame and massage them with lovely moisturiser afterwards. I will love and make them feel the best I can. I will embrace the amazing life I am so lucky to be living, the in love/hate relationship that we have!

May 25th

Everyone in this world is on a journey and has a story. Sometimes if we stop talking for long enough, and yes believe it or not I can, we are lucky enough to hear a bit of that story! I had a lovely time at the theatre last night and sat next to a young girl all on her own. In the interval she told me she that she was supporting her drama teacher on stage. She told me she had struggled from the age of eleven with her sexuality and that she was a lesbian. She carried on to say that she would have taken her own life at fifteen years old had it not been for her teacher on the stage. Her dad had been diagnosed with terminal cancer when she was also eleven with only three months to live; almost ten years later he had been given the all clear that very afternoon. It's funny how just in a few minutes you can learn so much about someone and how it can have a profound impact on you when you least expect it. I watched the second half seeing the drama teacher who was performing in a very different light.

May 26th

At the moment I have terrible trouble getting into the shower! Firstly, I can only shower with help, so when I come in from training I have to hang around in smelly gym gear until someone is free and that's not pleasant. It isn't the easiest of transfers getting in either. In the evening when my body is tired it's even worse. Quite often even with the brakes on, the shower chair slips, which is scary. The inflatable shower chair is also quite wobbly. I can't sit back properly and it puts a strain on my back, and I can't relax as I have the thought of trying to get out again hanging over me. That's even harder than getting in as I'm wet and it makes everything slippery. The most frustrating thing is having to have someone help me with this stressful process and see their frustration and hurt as they watch my struggle. A wet room alleviates everyone of these pressures and anxieties. I sit on my shower chair, wheel into my wet room and turn on the shower. Things couldn't be easier and what a pleasure my shower experiences will become instead of just a chore. I wouldn't consider jumping out of a plane for the fun of it. It makes my heart race just thinking of it, but I have to do something to raise the money for my wet room as I can't get a grant.

16.33

I may not be able to shower independently but I achieved another FIRST today. I can't get into the back garden but between 9-11am I have a little suntrap on my front doorstep. I've sat out quite often on sunny mornings and although it's lovely to enjoy the sun with a cup of tea and it would be perfect, I've been nervous about trying to carry one out with me. I need to navigate through three doorways, along a carpeted hallway and two steps with a cup of tea in hand, MASSIVE CHALLENGE for fear of spilling and burning myself. Today I took it very slowly, it took about ten minutes but hey look at me. The cat that got the cream! I asked Mr Postie to take a photo to capture my very happy proud moment!

20.30

My friend and Meg my eldest daughter are doing the tandem skydive with me and I'm so proud of Meg for wanting to support me on this scary venture. I hope you are able to support us, too.

> *The bit of sun in the front garden would set me up for the day. The thought of sitting in that corner would give me the incentive to face the struggle of getting up. Funny how I had never really even noticed that piece of front garden before and now it was my little piece of heaven on earth.*

May 27th

Just back from Jacob's last day at St Philip Howard High School. It's not possible that the school year for him is finished, let alone school life. It's been a tough school year for him, too, for all my children in fact. I was in hospital for six months of it. Although that seems forever ago it was a significant time in terms of a school year. I was lucky to be able to be at his last school assembly and felt very proud of him. Jacob stayed on to play football, so I'm embracing quality time with Amelia before she slips through my fingers and is finishing school, too.

> *I feel quite disjointed from school life with my children. It seems so much longer than just six months that I have been away as so much has happened. In that time Jacob has finished his last school year. The end of an era. I also guess I am coming back after a life-changing experience. I am just so thankful that my children have managed to keep their heads above water since I've been gone and carried on with their school work regardless. I thank God and the angels for watching over them while I was away. Just as someone watched over me the day of the accident.*

May 28th

Feeling on top of the world. Today was such a struggle to get up. I kept telling myself that as it was so bad the day could only get better. Boy did it ever! Furthest distance ever on my handbike – just over seven miles. The days that sometimes start off the worst, end up being the best!

> *When a day starts so bad, it can only get better. If it doesn't, then at least you can tell yourself that you have made the effort to get up – some people can't even do that.*

May 29th

Today has been a day of quiet reflection. A lovely morning spent with a beautiful family with two gorgeous young boys. Watching them play reminded me of my children when they were young and their quirky little ways. Life was just so carefree and full of fun. Today was the Arundel Triathlon. Two years ago it was my very first one. Last year I competed as part of a relay team with two lovely ladies, maybe next year I might do it again. I may need a bit of help from the pool to transistion. Last year I worried about running it without my glasses on for fear of bumping into something; I don't have that worry any more, I can no longer run! Finally, today we had our first BBQ of the year. The last one we had was the day before my accident and Rosie had her last BBQ sausage. Life is always changing and moving. Nothing stays the same and today I was reminded of that in many ways.

May 30th

I've had a 'pamper Bert and Ernie' afternoon. As I write this post, I would like to make it ABUNDANTLY CLEAR that I am NOT CRITICISING ANYONE who uses pain relief drugs to help manage their pain or condition. Pain is very personal to the individual and one must do what suits and makes life bearable for you. I chose to leave Stoke Mandeville on no pain relief drugs. I wanted to give my body as much chance as possible to sort its own pain management out. Most of the time I cope quite well but sometimes it is hard. Recently the neuropathic pain and spasms have got worse. In hospital I had access to a motorised cycling machine that I used daily. As I still have a few funds left in my pink wheelchair account, I've bought a cycling machine for use at home. I've also treated myself to a Tens machine. Stimulating old Bert and Ern should help ease their discomfort and the Tens machine will be very useful for my other aches and pains elsewhere, too.

May 31st

Isn't it funny how you go through life completely oblivious to some things until it actually concerns and affects you. I have never really paid much attention to a public disabled toilet before, yet now they are almost becoming a bizarre obsession. That is simply because the majority of ones that I visit are simply NOT disabled friendly. They are designed for people with limited mobility as far as I can tell. Not for someone with complete paralysis and no use of their legs at all. Quite often as you enter the toilet there is a large bin situated inside. Invariably this is stood on the side of the toilet with the most space. This is the side I need to wheel my chair. I have to pull this bin out of the way before I start negotiating my transfer onto the toilet. There is always a pull-down handle on the wall next to the toilet. Very helpful, but on the wrong side. It's always on the side on which I have to wheel my chair and then I can't pull it down because it blocks my transfer onto the toilet itself. I've also actually broken three public toilets with my transfers as they aren't designed for someone who has to rock from side to side to pull their trousers up. My legs don't work. They don't weight bear and quite often they swing freely as I'm too little to touch the floor. I can't use them to assist in any way. Pulling up trousers is great fun without legs! All in all, a trip to the toilet ends up being like a workout in the gym as I have to stretch and lean and pull and grab onto anything. On the odd occasion, I've almost ended up on the floor. Just as well I like a workout but I'm thinking of writing to the council to see if they are aware that their disabled toilets are more for the less-abled and maybe not for completely disabled people!

June 2016

June 2nd

I had two new experiences yesterday. Both affected me differently. Firstly, something that I've been contemplating for a while but didn't think I'd be strong enough because of the dead weight of my legs. This was attempting chin-up's on a bar. Very good for improving upper strength. I managed half a dozen or so on a bar in a park, even lifting the front wheels of my chair up with me. It left me on a high. Second experience.

My motor-powered peddling machine arrived. Bert and Ernie wouldn't stay in the straps so we put the cleat pedals from my racing bike on the machine and I attached myself with my cycling shoes. This was a very bittersweet experience. Never in my life did I think I'd wear my cycling shoes again after my accident. Although I am not peddling and the motor is doing the work it felt very peculiar watching my feet go round in my shoes. I kept flashing back to Bury Hill. The stimulation to Bert and Ernie did them the world of good but not sure about my mental well-being. I guess I'll get used to it in time! Time heals all wounds.

June 3rd

Feeling really excited and certain I am making a really good decision. Having been so lost without my Rosie dog and quite redundant without my guide dog puppy since I've been home, I discovered a scheme today for re-homing guide dog puppies. These are puppies who have failed training or working guide dogs who can no longer work. On applying there is no waiting list, the scheme works on compatibility. If a dog that matches the dog you have requested needs a home you could have one within a few weeks. If no dog is available for you after six months you have to apply again. My application is being posted as I type.

I decided that if I wanted to have a big dog then I would rather have one that was already trained rather than a puppy. I have volunteered with Guide Dogs for six years or so and never realised that they had a re-homing system. I can't wait to see what I might get.

June 4th

Well, other than jumping out of a plane in August I've just committed to my biggest adventure yet. Tickets booked for Meggie and I to travel to Ireland. A very long overdue visit to stay with my brother and his adorable family!

I'm quite nervous about the prospect of flying but there is no way I am going to let my disability restrict me from doing the things I want to do. I will just have to be prepared to go out of my comfort zone a little more in order to accomplish them. It is character building and I will feel really good for doing it.

June 6th

Being a mum of four children is quite a task normally I'd say. In a wheelchair its role is tested even further. I can cook meals but it's impossible to get things in and out of the oven independently. I still have no car, so can't even provide Mum's taxi service. I also know it's very hard on my children seeing me sitting in my wheelchair rather than rushing round like the headless chicken I was. My motherly role feels a little compromised at present and it's my favourite role in the whole world. This morning when one of my children comes in to say goodbye as they leave for school and tells me they've had a really lovely half-term holiday with me, it doesn't get any better. I feel on top of the world and couldn't wish for a better compliment than that!

17.20

I emailed the Worthing 10k director this year explaining how I had loved running the 10k last year, but was now in a wheelchair. I said I would still LOVE to participate with my handbike and would happily start at the back. I received an email refusing my entry on the grounds that the race had not been set up for wheelchair participation and that they couldn't change this rule just for me. Besides, there were a few curbs I may not manage and that they were very sorry. Never mind, plenty more races out there but I know this is going to happen a fair few times!

Us Mums always worry they are doing a good job. I feel this more than ever now and I know my accident has had a massive impact on my children especially now that I am home. Days are tough sometimes and I can feel the awkwardness between us. I think it is easier for my youngest two children. I feel that the older two are struggling more. They are teenagers and I think life in general is more of a struggle at that age and now they have this to contend with too. Things aren't going to change overnight but I know that we will work our way through this in our own time. I just need to be patient and it will happen.

It is also very hard accepting rejection for your disability when only a few months ago my entry for a race would have been accepted without question. I didn't ask for my accident to happen or to lose the use of my legs. It was a hand of fate that could happen to anyone. I also know that I could complete the Worthing 10k course but sometimes in life you just have to let things go and concentrate on the more important issues. In this case, building up relationships with my children is of paramount importance and next to it a race entry denial pales into insignificance. I have more important races to win with my children.

June 7th

What an absolutely brilliant day. Firstly, Nick Gibb has replied to my letter regarding disabled toilets. Secondly, a letter with a cheque attached was presented to me tonight at the Bognor Rotary dinner at Bognor Golf Club. I was privileged to be given an invitation as a special thanks for my part at the Bognor 10k. The cheque I received is to help go towards my pink racing bike. A pound for every race entry from the Bognor 10k was donated. I felt very emotional when I received it. Running meant so much to me, so to be given a pound from almost 1,400 runners was truly special and touching. I'm too excited to sleep!

After the rain the sun always comes out. I am finding this a lot since my accident. Good days always follow the tough ones. We have to sit through the rain and wait for the sun to come out again and it always does.

June 8th

Just watched this beautiful young lady ride off to take her first A-level exam in Psychology. No one could have worked harder than my Meg. She has had her head buried deep in books for weeks now, so I hope and pray she reaps the rewards of all her efforts.

June 9th

This morning I sat outside in the early sun just pondering over things. I have had so many wonderful things happen recently and there are so many wonderful things to come. Sometimes people ask me if I will ever walk again.

When I say no, they tell me how sorry they are. No one should feel sorry for me because although things may be hard at times, I am the happiest I have ever been. I wouldn't change my life for anything!

June 10th

Whilst enjoying an afternoon cream tea, a seven-month-old baby on the table opposite kept staring at me. I automatically assumed it was because of my wheelchair. I thought he was staring at that. After a while a conversation started with his mother. She informed me that he had a fascination with watches and shiny jewellery, hence the reason why she wasn't wearing any. He was staring at my watch. As we left I wheeled up to him and once in reach he nearly had the watch off my wrist! It really made me smile. Children are such accepting human beings. They have a beautiful innocence about them, and don't make judgements or see things as odd or strange. They just see them as they are.

June 11th

Today Amelia had her football presentation, it was just down the road. This meant I could take her as we could walk. It was our first outing together alone since my accident. This was a big challenge for both of us. Several times Amelia said she didn't want me to come. This hurt quite a lot but she had valid reasons. Amelia was worried about being out with me on her own. She was worried that I could get stuck in a rut on a pavement or couldn't get up a curb or, worse still, fall out of my chair. She was concerned about there being a disabled toilet at the venue, and also worried that I would be left on my own at football and that she would have to stay with me. All quite overwhelming responsibilities for a child. I wanted to show Amelia how independent I was, I didn't want her to have to look out for me. I felt a lot of pressure to prove myself and not let her down. Our journey began in complete

silence. The nearer to the tournament we got, the more the atmosphere between us became relaxed. Amelia apologised for being stroppy with me, but I told her I loved her and understood. Once at the tournament a lovely mum came straight over and invited me to sit with her and her family. Amelia gave me a massive hug and kiss and ran off to be with her friends. All responsibility was alleviated and she had the freedom to be a child once again. One of the best afternoons ever and we walked home together completely happy and relaxed. Another mountain climbed and conquered together.

A tough and important race with my child won today. Much better in my opinion than the Worthing 10k any day!

June 14th

Some days I feel quite 'rough'. Yesterday was one of those days. I'm not sure why really, I think it's just my body getting used to the whole new change. I think after living and doing things one way for forty-five years, suddenly only working with half a body is going to take some getting used to. Almost cancelled a night out with a lovely friend, too but so glad I didn't. Good company and lots of laughter are sometimes all the medicine you need! Oh, and of course a sticky pudding too – I've woken up feeling great.

June 15th

Really lovely country stroll and roll with Mike. I managed to christen the wheels with their first amount of dog poo! Well I guess it was inevitable that it would happen at some point!

June 16th

I treated Bert and Ernie to something extra special today. I bought them the most sparkly, glittery trainers you have ever seen. They interchange colour between gold and cerise pink! The best thing about them is that they will never wear out! It couldn't have rained any harder if it tried today; we got absolutely soaked but the weather just added to the fun! I think people kept staring at us because we were laughing so loudly. Laughter is so good for the soul. The really funny thing is, if you asked me what we were laughing about I couldn't tell you!

I can honestly say that I have laughed more than ever since my accident. I think that is because sometimes I choose to laugh rather than cry. I have to get through the challenges and upheavals of coming to terms with my disability somehow and I would much rather do it with a happy outlook and making light of it, than feeling sorry for myself and being miserable. People don't want to hang around with a miserable cow, either, and I certainly don't want to be lonely. I would have no one to talk to.

June 17th

Thank you from the bottom of my heart to all those who have helped and supported me so far. Please help me continue on my journey to the fullest amount of independence I can possibly have.

June 18th

Since my accident I have been lucky enough to try many different activities. Well, today I fell head over heels in love with this activity and the beautiful animals involved. I traded my two crippled, useless legs for four powerful ones. Horseriding made me feel normal. I did something in the same way as an able-bodied person. Plus the movement of the horse made me feel like I was walking. I was no longer little in my chair. I was on top of the world looking down, not up! My pony, Bird had a really rough start in life and was badly treated and abused. Look at her now. The most beautiful, sensitive little creature and she was so non-judgemental and accepting of me. I felt so at ease in her company, I can't wait to go again. Thank you so much Kerry for giving up your time and organising such a special day!

A day that I will remember for ever as it had such a profound impact on me. I had only ridden a couple of times as an able-bodied person and was pretty useless. The reason was due to the fact that I used my legs too much and used to grip too tightly with them to the horse. Now I didn't have the use of my legs I rode much better. I also felt that the horse and I became one and that I was walking through the horse. My body was simulating how I used to walk before I had my accident, and I could feel muscles working again. I really felt so emotional and that this was going to be the beginning of something truly special.

June 19th

This morning I had a visitor in my front garden. He was a little ninety-four-year-old man walking his dog and he just stopped to chat as I was sat drinking my tea. He didn't even know it was Father's Day! He had two sons, grandchildren and great grandchildren. His wife had died five years ago and his little dog Mitsey slept on her pillow. He thanked me for my time and bothering to talk to him. He also said he was pleased I seemed so happy. He said you might as well be six foot under if you are miserable. I spent the afternoon with two possible fathers-to-be. They helped me get some mileage in for the 401 marathon in October. Their company kept me going and made all the difference.

I thought of the old man. Companionship is so important, he told me where he lives. I might go and visit him this week and we can sit in his front garden and chat. The funny thing is his name is Bert!

June 21st

Lots of changes and things happening in life at present. A son wearing his uniform for the last time and a daughter leaving school for good on Thursday. Also, lots of events triggering memories for me when I was able-bodied. I think the novelty of leaving hospital has worn off and the reality of life is kicking in. It's also kicking in with a big difference. I am living life as a paraplegic. I've struggled a little the past few days but today I was able to put things back into perspective. Just sitting on the jetty with the stunning scenery in front of me was enough to make me realise how lucky I am and how beautiful my life is. We can't appreciate things all the time but there is no feeling like it when you take stock and it all becomes apparent to you again.

June 22nd

So far away are the nights when it was a bedtime story and a beaker of milk. Out tonight celebrating Megan's last exam and the end of her school days. In a few months' time this baby bird flies the nest for a new beginning and new adventures at university. I couldn't love her any more or be more proud of her.

June 23rd

I confess that I don't really have much of an idea about politics and all this 'in/out' business really unsettles me. So I ask my youngest just as he leaves for school who he would vote for. He delivers a very solid answer, supported with confident, very well-composed and thoughtful reasons. I see his logic and I'm proud and impressed that he has obviously researched his evidence and knows what he is talking about. It is his future that is ultimately going to be effected most by today, so I am going to vote with him and for him. Problem solved!

June 24th

I have blue sky and the sun shining in my window. I have four children pottering around getting ready for school. I have a cup of tea being brought up to me. I heard the kettle boil and now a spoon stirring sugar in a cup. I'm snuggled under my duvet safe and warm. Great Britain and the people who live in it have woken up this morning with a new future on the horizon. It's the unknown, but at this moment I am alive and well and happy with a nice day ahead. That is all I need right now and this moment is all I can guarantee. I will worry about tomorrow when it happens.

I guess one of my biggest concerns is how people with disabilities will be affected by all this change. To be honest, though, my accident has really taught me to only worry about the things I can change and to let go of the things I can't. So this is exactly what I am going to do.

June 25th

The sun is shining again and the birds are singing. The world is still revolving. Yesterday I had my first real injury below my sensation level since my spinal accident. There was blood. It was scary because I didn't know where it was coming from. I found it quite quickly. I'd taken a chunk out of my heel. Goodness knows how it happened but if I could feel, I know that it would hurt. It is a very funny feeling knowing you have hurt yourself but can't feel the pain. Some would say make the most of that but personally I don't like it. Pain is natural and your body's way of alerting you something is wrong. I can't change this, though. I think it's very important in life, especially at the moment, to find the serenity to accept the things we can't change, the courage to change what we can and the wisdom to know the difference – a very profound quote indeed!

I am feeling a little wobbly about my injured heel. Cuts and knocks and bruises are so much more serious with a spinal injury. I know how quickly it can turn into something nasty and I can't feel it at all. I also can't stop

Bert from spasming and knocking it further. I am willing it to heal as quickly as possible. My circulation is compromised, so the healing process may take even longer. To me this is my biggest concern at the moment. All I am going to attempt to do is accept the fact that I can't control my legs from spasming and that I can no longer feel pain. I can control keeping a close eye on my foot by wearing socks to give it protection and seeking medical advice if I become overly worried that it isn't healing well enough on its own. I have also found the wisdom to know the difference between what I can and can't control.

June 26th

What a fab day! Went to boot camp this morning and managed to climb halfway up a 14-foot rope unaided. Then horseriding again in the afternoon. I managed to balance for well over a minute with no hands. This may sound easy but I remember the days in the gym where I could only sit on my own on a plinth for a few seconds with my trusty sick bowl by my side. Today I managed it on a horse. Feeling so happy with my life.

June 27th

A visit to a disabled department in a school later today with a view to helping the children with sport after the summer holidays. Visiting Fareham my guide dog puppy tomorrow and sending her on her way to her final training. A chance to see the re-homing puppies, too. Off to Ireland next Thursday. Parachute jump ever looming and hoping to learn to scuba dive. I hope to get my PADI Open Water qualification in Mexico next May. There is also the slight matter of a marathon in October. I can't wait to meet up with Ben Smith from the 401 challenge again. Life holds so many opportunities for you whoever you are and whatever your capabilities. You just have to want them, go looking for them and take them! I think my life is fuller and more exciting now than ever. I hurt all over today (well, what I can feel) but can't wait to shake it all off and get going. Cup of tea first though, of course!

20.06

Lying with Bert and Ernie safe and under control at last! Today didn't go quite as well as I had planned. The cut on Bert began weeping. Having paralysed limbs that spasm and feel pain which I can no longer feel in my head, is like having two young babies. That's why I named them. I have to look after them, determine what is going on by sight, intuition, judgement and I guess maybe maternal instinct. I was worried about the infection as it was yellowish in colour. I managed to get a nurse's appointment for the afternoon. In the meantime Ernie got stuck under the seat in a friends car. He could feel he was stuck and something was hurting him so he spasmed and the metal on the seat stuck into my ankle and made that

bleed. It's horrible seeing it happen but not being able to reach out and stop it. It's similar to watching a child, knowing something is hurting them, which is upsetting. I just think to myself, you silly things please stop hurting yourselves. Luckily there was no infection. The yellow was just old dead cells dropping off in liquid form. I have had both cuts cleaned and dressed and protected with plasters. Made me chuckle, as again as with a child, a plaster makes everything better. Sometimes, though, having four children already I don't want two more to look after. It's a big responsibility! On the bright side, however, I got to eat two portions of chips and an ice cream with fantastic lovely friends. They helped look after me and my unpredictable legs today. Without such great friends it would be a million times harder!

June 28th

Such a beautiful day with lots of very special dogs. One in particular of course, my lovely Fareham. Fareham has a sore toe at the moment so is on rest. That suited us as we just got to have loads of cuddles rather than watching her work. She did show us how she puts on her own harness. This is a great help to a visually impaired person. I'm hoping so much that a guide dog is going to come up for re-homing. No chance of sneaking one home today though!

June 29th

Last night I was too tired and sore to transfer into the shower I'm using at present. This morning I'd love to be able to have a shower to help get me going. I can't. With my new wet room I'll have the ease and freedom to shower as I wish. People are being so supportive and helpful regarding helping me get my wet room. Please, please continue with your support to get my independence back and please keep sharing. Thank you.

21.06

I had all the sunshine I could wish for today. I got sent a beautiful sunshine picture from Greece. My baby bird is enjoying her first holiday abroad with her boyfriend Tom. It melted my heart to see her looking so happy! Lots of beautiful prom photos tonight on Facebook, too. I hope Sophia and Jacob have a lovely time and I can't wait for the pictures to follow. Our babies grow so quickly.

June 30th

OMG – feeling so excited! A letter from Parliament yesterday and a phone call just now from some minister (not sure who as the letter with his name on is downstairs), BUT regarding disabled toilets and the government's plans for updating them. There are occupational therapists involved and the minister is getting me involved too. I may perhaps sit in on meetings and help with planning! It certainly pays off sometimes to make an effort to get things changed. I'm so glad that my little amount of effort may have an effect on other people's lives whilst out and about and making the use of toilets a little bit easier.

13.25

So from toilet designing to something a lot more glamorous. Beautiful pictures of my handsome boy that were worth waiting for. They make me gasp and take my breath away. So young and happy with a whole life ahead, the journey is just beginning.

July 2016

July 1st

Wow, wow, wow! How often do you get a tank come down your road! How lucky was I to be allowed to sit on it. A really fab day today! Got my dressing changed on my foot and it's healing nicely – best news ever. Joe got to skate at The Base. Bought a new lightweight suitcase for Ireland, too, and ended my afternoon with the tank and my boy! Joe was absolutely made up and almost as excited as me.

> *It was such a relief that my foot was really healing. All of a sudden the weight of the worry was gone and the day was just full of happiness and special times.*

July 3rd

Maybe whilst I help design disabled toilets for the country, I can design my own wet room too!

14.36

A truly memorable and special day today. Met up with Gill at the British Heart Foundation bike ride at the Goodwood racetrack. We met here two years ago and cycled together for a while. Quite a lot has happened since we first met. Today was a very special day to see Gill again. I met the organiser of the event and apparently I'm the first wheelchair entry the event has seen since it started eighteen years ago.

I can't believe that! I thought loads of wheelchair users would see it as a fabulous opportunity to burn some rubber. I'm hoping now that I've done it, more wheelchair users will consider participating in it. Today I anticipated getting up to ten miles. Well I miscounted and did six laps. That equates to almost fourteen and a half miles! My Joe says that I should feel really proud. Do you know what, I really am!

> *I just pootled round Goodwood today but I was in such a good headspace I completed lap after lap with ease. Exercise is all about positive mental attitude, something I lacked a lot in my running, but which I seem to have lots of now in my new life. Funny how things change. In a way you would expect it to have been the other way around.*

July 4th

Swimming is something I really would like to get back to doing. I love hydro but I miss swimming as exercise. I need help, though, because I'm not sure what my legs are going to do in the water. They may sink, they may float. They are pretty temperamental and water temperature has a big impact, too. If it is too cold they spasm badly. It looks like I may have found just what I need, a swimming session at the Chichester pool called Otters. It might be just what I need to help me get back into the water again!

> *I am really keen to swim again but have so much else going on. Otters in Chichester sounds like a fantastic place to start. I guess I should not worry too much about it, it will happen when it happens, but I do feel a real desire to swim again at some point. I've learnt that some things you think you will do straight away you just don't and then you also end up doing things you never dreamed of. That is the great thing about life – it is full of constant surprises.*

July 5th

Sunshine and sushi before hydro. I have become very close to Verity my hydro physio. We have to work together on a very personal level. We work very well together with the same perspective on things. We also work very hard. I always have a tiny bit of hope that one day I may walk again. No one knows anything for sure. I am a very firm believer in working with the gifts that you have, I have hip flexors that are showing flickers of activity and getting stronger weekly. I didn't have this after my accident. If I concentrate really hard I can engage them. Today I sat in a chair in the water. I practised trying to engage each hip flexor one at a time to lift my leg. This is a massive ask of one tiny muscle to pull a great big leg up. I can't engage my quads as that would really help. I won't give up, though. I'm so lucky with the amount of movement that I do have. Verity says the flexors have definitely got stronger. I will continue to push myself with what I have, and anything else I gain in the process is a plus.

July 6th

Oooooh, how exciting. I've volunteered to help at the London World Championship Athletics in 2017 and I've had a mention in the volunteers so far! It would be amazing to actually be chosen. Thank you, Helen!

July 7th

Feeling pretty anxious, about to leave for the airport and travel to Ireland. I have phoned and informed easyJet that I am disabled and need assistance. I told the man on the phone that I'm in a wheelchair and paralysed from the waist down. He then asks me if I can walk up the aisle to my seat! Um, oh dear – I think this is going to be interesting. More nervous than ever now!

18.20

I can't walk but I CAN FLY! I've arrived safely! Apart from accidently setting off the alarm in the disabled toilet and causing a bit of a stir it was fine. Feel tired as I've had to concentrate so hard on what was going on and what I had to do, but now the world's my oyster.

It's not only a physical tiredness that I feel adapting to my new life in my wheelchair; it is mentally exhausting too. For forty-five years I did everything one way and it was all natural. I didn't have to think about a lot of things, I just did them. I would walk up a step or curb without noticing it was even there. Now if there is a step or curb, I have to re-

plan my whole route around them. I no longer have my hands free for carrying things and that makes such a big difference. I have to think about where to put things and how to make them easily accessible and where I can get to them quickly. It is just silly little things that you take for granted that I can no longer do. Carrying hot drinks or liquids is a task as well these days. Do I carry the milk to the cereal bowl or the bowl to the milk? At the airport I actually found myself watching able-bodied people a lot more. Lots of people jiggle their legs up and down without realising it whilst sitting down, and some climb stairs with ease maybe taking two steps at a time. In a way I resented them having their legs and I also resented them for not really appreciating them. I only appreciate walking because I can no longer do it. Like everything associated with a spinal injury, this is just another thing I have to accept and a hurdle to overcome, and although I can no longer physically jump over hurdles, I'm getting quite good at leaping over metaphorical ones.

July 9th

Having just the best family time ever in Ireland. I have three adorable nieces who provide hours of entertainment. Children have the best perspective on things. Hannah, who is two, loves my bike.Sophia, four and Ella, six, love wheeling around in my chair! My brother has made his house completely wheelchair friendly for me. A ramp out the front and drop-down hand rail in the toilet, on the correct side for me to transfer. My sister-in-law has spoilt Meg and I with amazing home-cooked healthy food. We
are lying on the bed at the moment awaiting home-made melanzane parmigiana. I think my trips to Ireland are going to become frequent!

It's quite ironic that I was worried Ade would not have made any preparations for me coming over to stay. I couldn't have been more wrong. It was quite emotional for me to see all the effort he had gone to ensuring that my stay would be a pleasurable and enjoyable one. Again it just illustrated how much I was really loved and how lucky I was to have people in my life who really cared for me.

July 10th

I really am treasuring my time here in Ireland. The children are just such a breath of fresh air. Little Hannah is so accepting of my chair she will never remember me as being any other way. It's like being in a little bubble where the most important thing in your world is doing headstands on the sofa!

Ella and Sophia both drew me a picture. Both of them had drawn me standing without my wheelchair. I asked Sophia first where my wheelchair was – she told me it wasn't there because she couldn't draw them. I then asked Ella the same question. She replied that she hadn't drawn the wheelchair because she wanted me to get better and not have to use one.

July 12th

Delayed and grumpy at Belfast airport. My back hurts from just sitting around. Next time I'm on a plane I will be jumping, well falling, out of it! At least I have my Meggie here for company and have had the best few days ever!

20.56

Every cloud has a silver lining – free hot chocolates courtesy of easyJet and extra time spent with my precious girl, time that I wouldn't have had if the flight hadn't been delayed.

Going home was so much more relaxing than coming. Although Meg and I had a delay we were much more relaxed together. Meg was a lot more confident with me being in my chair as she knew what to expect now. It did our relationship the world of good. Every day little steps and today was quite a big one.

July 13th

Stuck in traffic when I get a lovely surprise message from my baby girl. So proud of Amelia Worne and can't wait to give her a massive hug when I get home.

July 14th

Almost home and at last I can share my exciting news! A few weeks ago I was chosen to be an ambassador for a campaign called 'Together We Will'. This campaign is aiming to encourage people of all disabilities to become active in any way, shape or form. Eight national disabled sporting organisations have come together to try and make this happen, as so many disabled people do not take part in any physical activity. They have also been joined by the English Federation of Disability Sport. The idea is to also encourage the activity to involve family and friends. Hence the title 'Together We Will'. Will Mellor is also involved as an abassador as his sister was disabled and he helped teach her to ride a bike. This led to her having enough confidence to go to college. Today I was in Manchester for the official launch. We had interviews and photos with the BBC and various other media organisations. Initially, the campaign will last for three months. During this time I will be recording my activities and my day-to-day life. This again will then receive various forms of media coverage. I know this is a long entry but I just feel so proud, privileged and honoured to not only support this campaign, but to be a major spokesperson for it. I have the opportunity to be a big influence in hopefully helping people with disabilities become involved in sport, and experience the same happiness and joy it gives to me in so many different ways. Today has been the best day ever and a big thank you to Lydia for putting up with me and being my chauffeur and a big support throughout.

July 15 18.46

This was on Manchester TV. Please share if you will to really help this campaign to encourage people with disabilities to get active.

Being chosen for the 'Together We Will' campaign filled me with such pride and gave me such a confidence boost. Going up to Manchester and meeting Will Mellor was such an experience too. It was all such a whirlwind of events and a bit of a blur dashing from place to place for photo shoots but such great fun. A little disappointing as we were supposed to be on ITV's breakfast show but Theresa May became Prime Minister and she stole my spot! I feel I have an important role to play now too, promoting sport and activity to people with disabilities. I am looking forward to what I think is going to be quite an active couple of months.

July 16th

At long last two pink wheels finally has her four blue wheels. A lovely surprise, and a bunch of flowers as well because of the delay. The road to freedom is mine. Anyone need a lift?

It feels like my life is really coming together at the moment. My car is just absolutely beautiful. I can hardly believe that it actually belongs to me. Never did I think that I would be the owner of a brand new car straight out of the factory, but here I was and it was true. Joe said to me as we drove home that it was almost worth being disabled as you got a new car. I turned round to him with a big grin and said it actually is worth being disabled to get car. That, along with all the other lovely experiences I was having, I wouldn't have swapped any of it for the world – let alone a pair of working legs!

July 17 09.11

From the waist down my body is numb and fizzing. From the waist up it hurts all over! Yesterday with some amazing friends and my beautiful daughter I was able to complete a really difficult hilly and muddy five-mile race. The race director altered the course slightly for us to accomodate me. Even so, the first hill was almost as steep and long as the Trundle. It took us over an hour but it was simply the best race ever. My friends helped push me up the steep sections. They held onto to me for dear life on the downward sections that were too steep for the brakes to hold me. Bearing in mind the

nature of my accident I put all my trust in them not to let anything happen and they didn't let me down! The campaign 'Together We Will' promotes disabled people getting active with the support of others. Yesterday was a prime example of people working together and supporting me, helping me to achieve whatever I want. I value my friends and family more than anything. Together We Will and Together We Did!

July 18th

Today I've done something that in my opinion is the bravest thing to date. I've taken off my anti-tips. I can't have complete independence in my car with them on my chair. They are awkward and I can't lift my chair into the car on my own with them on. It defeats the object of having a car and total independence. Now I'm nervous I'll tip back and crack my head open. I don't exactly have the best track record where accidents are concerned. I remember only too well what it feels like to be very broken. But it has to be done. Like taking stabilisers off your child's bike. They may fall off but their confidence increases and their independence will soar. I also discovered today the blood tests I had weeks ago confirmed a vitamin D deficiency. The doctors surgery just failed to tell me!

I've had a lot of joint pain in my elbows and felt pretty tired a lot of the time. This would explain why! Vitamin D supplements from tomorrow. I've found today pretty tough but had a few hours this afternoon at my family home. I was able to drive Amelia Worne and Joe over for a swim. Some days may not always be the best but there is always some good to be found in each day. These two smiley faces today were priceless!

July 19th
Well, low and behold, I survived my first day with no anti-tips. I didn't tip out backwards and bash my head either! A brilliant hydro session. Again I tried to engage my hip flexors to lift Bert (my right leg) when Ernie (my left leg) started doing it all on its own. My physio said if she didn't know better she would think I was a fraud! The weather is glorious, I have a car, my kids are fab. Life is wonderful and tomorrow I get to do it all again.

July 20th
Thank you to all my fantastic friends who have been so kind and supportive. I also know a few who are organising some fundraising after my jump. Thank you so much as well! Three weeks to go and I am getting nervous. I'm so lucky to have my car, just need my wet room now, well that and my dog!

July 21st
Still in bed thinking about how much I took for granted before my injury. Getting my car has been something I have looked forward to so much. I thought I'd get it and, hey presto, independence and freedom would be mine, mine, MINE! Well, like everything with a spinal injury there is always a challenge. I have realised the pain and tenderness in my elbows is caused by my driving. Up until now I have been the passenger and it was a chance when I could sit and rest my arms. Now of course I use them when I am driving. Using the hand controls takes a lot of repetitive hand movement and my tendons have become inflamed. I am quite tense too at the moment as I am still quite nervous about being back on the road, and yes, I am sure others are nervous about that, too! As my elbows are so sore I am struggling lifting my wheelchair in the car by myself as well. Obviously things will get easier and as with everything else in the spinal injury world, you overcome the obstacles and hurdles. Gone are the days,

though, when I just got into my car and drove and didn't give it a second thought! I will make sure that when I drive pain-free and with ease, I will always remember how lucky I am to have my independence.

18.02

Well I took today at 90mph rather than my usual 110mph. I spent some really special quality time with very special people. I also discovered a little resting place in my car for my sore elbow. It made the world of difference! I also managed to get my knickers caught on my transfer board getting out the car as I was wearing a dress. I got stuck halfway across the board and couldn't understand why! When I looked down I saw a very stretched pair of knickers stuck over the corner of the board. Thank God they didn't rip! We are encouraged at rehab to transfer without boards. I wonder if this is the reason why!

Really gutted about my right elbow. Isn't it always the way. When something is going so well, something else has to come along to upset the balance a bit. I can't even lift the kettle or brush my hair. We have a beautiful little bunny who lives under the stairs, and when I come down in the morning I wheel past him to a litle table on which sits my hairbrush and make-up. I always say hello to him on my way past, open the cage and give him a good fuss. He just shuts his eyes and laps it up. This morning with my arm being so sore and hair brushing so painful I spent a little longer fussing my little friend. It may sound silly but it was the most comforting feeling ever. I am not sure who enjoyed it most, the giver or the receiver.

July 22nd

Today saw the end to the toughest school year my children will ever have. I was in hospital for half of it. In a way I'm glad to put it all behind me. Joe started a whole new chapter of his life without me there to support him. Yet despite this, they have all made me feel so extremely proud with all their achievements. This summer holiday will be extra special. Last year it was cut short suddenly and abruptly with

no warning and I guess some might say quite tragically. I want to make a real effort to make this summer holiday extra, EXTRA enjoyable. Nothing big, nothing flash, just those little things that can often be taken for granted but actually mean so much.

July 23rd
Really enjoying the sun with this one! I cherish being a mum SO MUCH! It's the best job in the world by far.

> *Most summer holidays I would worry about trying to fill the days with exciting things to do. This year, as long as the sun shone and I was with my children, I didn't give two hoots what we did, I was just enjoying their company and time. Two of the most precious gifts we have.*

July 24th
Massive achievement today! Got my wheelchair out of the car all on my own, well, until a kindly gentleman INSISTED on helping put the second wheel on; theoretically this is something I have now mastered. Another step closer to independence. Amelia and I had a fun, girly shopping today. We also braved the car wash, got to keep my new car shining! We also had to take her broken glasses in for repairing. Amelia has just said she is off to her friends on her bike, NOT WITHOUT GLASSES she isn't! I'm tired and would rather not go out as my elbows still hurt but I remind myself of the frustrating months of not being able to help. I am really fortunate now that I can give my children lifts and be 'mum's taxi service' again. Crank up the tunes and have a blast!

July 25th
Lying on the bed covered in towels. Trying to compose myself after a pretty challenging bathing ordeal. Many people this morning would have had a 'quick' shower before work. Firstly, before I even contemplate a bath, I have to move a number of objects so I can transfer into the bath. In our bathroom there is not enough room to swing a cat let alone a wheelchair! This resulted in me knocking half a dozen items onto the

floor. Easy to pick up if you can stand and just bend. A lot harder sitting, bending down in a chair. Finally in the bath and Bert and Ernie are having none of it. Like grubby kids, apparently they were happy to stay dirty. So many spasms meant I was slip sliding around all over the place trying to stay upright. I tried to wash my hair one-handed. I needed to hold myself up with my other arm holding a grab rail. I managed to soak the whole bathroom with the shower and ended up with masses of soap in my eyes. With Bert and Ernie still fighting me the whole time, I admitted defeat and got out. My twelve-year-old had to assist as the shower chair kept slipping accross the floor. Not the greatest start to his day helping his mum in all her glory. A wet room eliminates so many of these problems. Life would be simply amazing and so much easier with one in my house.

20.52

In two weeks' time it will be a year since my accident. I would love it more than anything to have that Facebook year made into a book. Is there anyone out there amongst my lovely friends who could possibly help me?

Today was a really fundamentally important day in my life and the reason why I am writing this book. On asking if I could get a book printed of my adventures in a wheelchair, I found myself in receipt of a message from an old school friend asking if I had ever considered writing a proper book that could be published. Well, the rest is history and here it is. My very own book!

July 26th

Well, yesterday was another fab day. I went to a fun park in Sompting. The park started a scheme called 'We Cycle Too'. Unfortunately, though, the scheme hasn't really taken off. There is a tin shed full of about twenty bikes for disabled people that are hardly used. There is also a cycle track all ready built and just waiting for bikes. I met Matt. He helps run a charity called Wheels For All. This is a national inclusive cycling charity. We are hoping to get the park's 'We Cycle

Too' up and running again. It was very exciting to be part of this venture, such potential for people with disabilities to have a lot of fun. It is a very good example of how the 'Together We Will Campaign' works. Everyone is coming together to try and help as many people with disabilities as possible. Today, though, I am doped up to the eyeballs on diazepam, no driving for me. I've never had it before but boy I'm in a very happy little bubble feeling very drunk.

My goodness, I will never forget the diazepam episode for a trapped spasming nerve in my back. To be told to take 5mg not once, but twice, one at lunch and one at bedtime, led to me being on the phone in a terrible state to the doctor's the next morning. I felt almost suicidal. The comedown was like nothing I had experienced before. I was sat at the top of my stairs on the phone sobbing. I had never experienced anything like this at Stoke Mandeville. If they were putting you on a new drug you started on a tiny dose to see how you reacted. Maybe in hindsight, this should have been the case here too. Again, another lesson learned. As a result I was instantly told not to take any more and a bottle of morphine was prescribed instead. I think people with spinal injuries face a lot of issues with the medication they are on because of the side effects many of them have. Some make you feel really lethargic and dopey, some make you put on weight. One of my friends at Stoke Mandeville was on so much medication it made him dribble and I felt so sad for him. Lucky for me I only take a laxative to keep the old digestive system moving, vitamin D, and oxybutynin to stop bladder spasms. My understanding of this is so that when my bladder is full it doesn't spasm and send urine back up into my kidneys and round my body, which could be quite dangerous. It also helps prevent leaks. It makes my mouth quite dry, but in a way this is good as it encourages me to drink more, which I guess starts the cycle and need for the tablet all over again.

July 27th

I took diazepam before I went to bed and boy did it give me weird and wonderful dreams. I dreamt I was back at Stoke Mandeville having more rehab. We were in a big garden and some of the patients with a different injury from me were learning to take steps. I thought I would have a go. I stood up in my chair and low and behold Bert and Ernie took off and there was no stopping them. They just ran and ran and the only way to stop was to grab hold of things as I flew past them! I reckon I could have given Usain Bolt a run for his money. I got told I would still need my chair as I had no control of stopping myself. My turning wasn't great, either. It felt quite bizarre waking up as the dream felt so vivid. For a minute I thought it was real. I guess I feel a bit deflated and a bit tearful. How lovely would it have been to get out of bed and run to the bathroom! It's mornings like this when it's really important that I focus hard on how lucky I am despite not being able to walk. I have my four children all tucked up safely still asleep in their beds. I can hear a dog barking outside and know that I have the prospect of getting a dog again to look forward to. I have my arms and a full working brain, so I am able to share my thoughts on Facebook, and I have a new day ahead. I am seeing a very close friend later for a cuppa and she is bringing lunch. Tonight I am also going out for a meal with another lovely friend. How can I feel sorry for myself when my life is so rich and I have so much more than many.

July 28th

I tried to cancel this event today because I felt groggy and didn't want to drive because my elbow hurt. That didn't work because Dids insisted on picking me up. She had made a cake especially! I am so glad she did! What an ABSOLUTELY AMAZING DAY! I absolutely loved the experience of kayaking. Such a brilliant sport and it didn't hurt my elbow. I even went completely out of my comfort zone and capsized the kayak on purpose. That was really scary. Not being able to feel my legs and turning upside down in the water in a boat, and having to get myself out, BUT I DID IT! Thank you too David for being so patient and calm and believing in me.

July 29th

I had such a blast kayaking yesterday. I think it just illustrates that when you have the right support and encouragement you can achieve all your dreams. I'm hoping to go on the river soon, its exactly what the #TogetherWeWill campaign is aiming for.

16.29

OMG, this status gave me goosebumps! I did go back down Bury Hill again, but I came back up in an ambulance – but I wouldn't change a thing!

> **1 Year Ago**
> **See Your Memories**
> Amanda Newton
> **July 29th**
> Another boring bike status I'm afraid! Such a great ride IN THE SUN and 41.3mph down Bury Hill! I wanted to go back up and do it again, I'm turning into a speed junky!
> I'm happy that Hever Castle Triathlon training is going well.

It's funny but going up and down Bury Hill since my accident doesn't really bother me or stir up any emotion. It's often not the big things that upset me but smaller things, and it is when you least expect it. Seeing a post pop up from a year ago referring to Bury Hill caught me off guard. It didn't upset me though, it just made me shudder. It was the last time I would go down that hill to the bottom. I had no idea when I wrote that post of what was waiting round the corner for me the next time. It makes me cringe to think of what I was going to experience and the pain I would feel hitting the post. I guess I don't really even see the accident as an upsetting event anyway because I survived. It is just part of my life and an event that was meant to happen. I don't feel there is any reason to be upset by it as it has brought me to the happy place I am in today.

July 30th

Nice to see my new life still involves the 'bling'. Five medals already after only six months out of hospital. I'm looking forward to filling my medal rack up with exciting times ahead – anything is possible.

17.07

Just over a week to go and I AM JUMPING OUT OF A PLANE! Why jump out of a perfectly good plane you may ask? I am raising money for my wet room. Please help me get my independence back and make my leap of total madness worthwhile! Thank you so much.

July 31st

I know I may go on a bit, but life is our most precious and fragile gift! Today saw thousands of cyclists take part in the London Prudential bike ride. Some of those cyclists never completed the course. There were several horrific accidents. I was very lucky and completed the ride two years ago. My London Prudential cycling T-shirt had to be cut off me on the day of my accident while I was being given oxygen. Today I met an amazing and most kind-hearted man with an equally amazing story to tell. He came down from Crawley and gave me my chance to cycle again. He has just given me the most beautiful bike I could possibly dream of. He had been told of my accident and felt that I would really have some great fun with the bike. The only condition is that I ride to 10 Downing Street with him to meet the new Prime Minister! My life is just so fantastic and full and not a day goes by when I don't thank God for how flipping lucky I am!

August 2016

August 1st

Facebook comes up with some beautiful things sometimes. I awoke this morning to a 'Discover Your Story' photographic slideshow compilation. It sums up my life perfectly. 'Wonderful life and surrounded by good friends'.

August 2nd

Just a week to go. Hope the weather gets slightly better. JUMPING OUT A PLANE, EEEEK!

20.48

As it is just a week until the anniversary of my accident, the events of that day are very prominent in my mind. Today I phoned Brighton hospital. I got in touch with the resus nurse who cared for me when I came in off the ambulance. He was called Adam and had a great Australian accent. I remember him and I having a real blast. I kept being very sick. Shock and trauma I guess. He called me pukey Joe. I also remember him giving me loads and loads of morphine. There were lots of trauma nurses caring for me as I was in quite a bad way, but I remember Adam in particular. He was really pleased to hear from me, he hadn't forgotten me – funny that! I wanted to say a massive thank you to him for getting me stabilised. I wanted to tell him that although I had been so broken I was on the mend and enjoying life to the full. Hopefully there will be more to this. I'm hoping to meet up with him and some of the other nurses and maybe speak at a Trauma Training Day.

I was absolutely delighted that Adam remembered me. He must see hundreds of people come through his department, as treating them in the trauma unit is his job. He surely cannot remember them all, so it was brilliant that he recalled treating me. He played such an important role in my recovery. He was the first person to make me feel safe after my traumatic time lying in the bushes waiting to be found. I felt really poorly in the ambulance and very on edge because we were driving further away from my children. I requested to be taken to St Richards hospital in Chichester but I was in an ambulance that came from Worthing, so I had to go to Brighton. I was also still in a lot of pain. Adam eased my pain and helped me feel relaxed. In a way he was my lifeline at that point and he will always be a significant person even in years to come.

August 3rd

I really think this place is a little piece of heaven on earth. It is just stunning and so peaceful and beautiful. Today I had my first physio appointment since I left Stoke six months ago. A lot of my aches and pains are due to 'overloading'. My body has gone through a massive change including the trauma it had to overcome initially. Apparently I need to try and be... I think the word I am looking for but not familiar with is 'patient'. It is going to take time for me to gain all the strength I need in my upper body for my hectic life. It will come, but I need to build up to it gradually. I can't think of a better place to take things easy and not overload than here!

I think some people may perceive life in a wheelchair to be easier than it actually is. I think before my accident I was one of these people. The human body has to make a massive adjustment to functioning in a totally unnatural way and the whole body becomes compromised. It has to work a lot harder to compensate for what it has lost. Organs have to function differently, bowel and bladder have to be worked manually as they can no longer function on their own and that is very invasive for them. I also broke eleven bones and three vertebrae – one so badly that it was removed. I have a fair amount of metal work now too, which affects the body. I broke seven ribs and had one removed in surgery, which again is something your body never really recovers from. I hurt all the time and I feel more tired than I used to.

In a way I feel like my body has aged about ten years overnight and ironically a spinal injury shortens life expectancy by about ten to fifteen years. Then there is the physical exertion that I put on my upper body now every day when I move about in my chair. My arms act as my legs and have to do all the lifting. I find myself overstretching continuously in a world that isn't designed for people sat at about 4ft high in a wheelchair. Life is tough physically and then there are the mental challenges. People you meet not knowing how to behave around you. Trying to explain to people how you like things done politely. Letting people help you and do things for you when you have always been totally independent, accepting the things you can no longer do and having to compromise your choices and freewill. It's not surprising that some people with a spinal injury turn into recluses. For me, though, it is now just something I accept and want to get on with. I won't let it get me down and I am pleased that I am able to give other able-bodied people a real inside glimpse at what it is really like to live with a disability. I hope as a result that they will become more understanding and able to relate to others they meet who may also have a disability, without being uncomfortable or frightened of what to say and do.

August 4th

A few people have asked how I'm feeling with my year anniversary fast approaching. I feel really emotional today. Last year I posted a walk to Halnaker Windmill. I went with a very good friend. My Rosie dog came too. Since that day my four-legged friend has passed away and I lost the use of my two legs as well. Today I miss being able to go on walks, I miss barefoot running on the beach and sand between my toes. This time last year I only had four days left to enjoy these things. I wonder what I would have done if I'd known then what was around the corner. Probably been scared out of my mind and panic stricken. I think I would have stayed in bed to try and avoid it happening! It's lucky we can't see into the future really. Things happen, life changes and we deal with it. The thought of some things are so often worse than the reality. We worry too much about things that actually don't need worrying about. I have really learnt that in such a big way.

The last few days leading up to the anniversary of my accident was such a tumultuous, emotional affair. I was reminiscing on lots of lasts that I had done at that point in time a year earlier. Things that I would never ever do again, yet in the same breath it marked so many amazing achievements and so many new firsts. They were all coming together for a grand finale of what I would say was the most amazing year I had ever had.

August 5th

Today I gained such a really fundamental insight as to why the #TogetherWeWill campaign could, and hopefully will, make a real difference to other people with disabilities. Today I had the chance to meet up with two great guys and try my handbike out for the first time. Many mornings I wake up and it's hard to get going. Today I woke up with the worst stomach ache ever plus real aches and pains in my back, arms and shoulders. I had an incentive to get up, though. I had an exciting morning planned. Once settled in my bike and speeding round the track I soon forgot my ailments. The sun was hot on my sore shoulders and lying in my bike eased my tummy, allowing me to stretch. Plus the movement loosened up lots of tight muscles. With the wind blowing gently on my brow I felt awesome. What a difference from how I felt first thing. People with all sorts of disabilities have different ailments and challenges to face daily, too. If they are not fortunate to have an activity to participate in they may just spend the day indoors. This just accentuates how awful they may feel; without the help of others they may not be able to get out. My activity made me feel on top of the world today. That's why it's so important that I do my best to help others have the opportunities to be active, too.

August 6th

Really special morning spent with this wonderful man. Coffee and cake at the top of Bury Hill this year though, not a meeting with me broken and buried in bushes at the bottom. I really think I would not be here without Gary. We drove down to the spot where he found me. He told me how I was completely

hidden from view. It was only my cries that alerted him of my whereabouts! I feel so thankful today that he rode past, and we had lots of laughs as well as some reflective moments. We even joked about checking to see whether I'd dropped any money last year and about looking to see if we could find it. Feeling really reflective today having revisited the scene. It's a bloody great day to be alive!

> *Just a very surreal day about how friendships can be formed in the most unexpected places. Gary and I would never have met had it not been for my accident. Fate had thrown us together and here we were a year on with a very special relationship that isn't experienced by many, and him and I are the only ones who have a real concept of how that day had such an impact on us both.*

August 7th

How exciting. Sitting at the poolside waiting to take part in my first Triathlon. The atmosphere is buzzing and so am I. Up at 5am, which is the earliest since my accident. Bert and Ernie didn't know what had hit them. I am in a relay team with Judith and Paul. I'm watching Judith on the swim. Paul is doing the bike ride and I'm doing the run of course!

12.05

Wow! What a way to start your Sunday. So very grateful to those who made it possible for me to participate in the Bognor Triathlon this morning. I felt so chuffed to be part of a great team with Judith and Paul. Lovely people and amazing athletes who supported me on the run too. I'm blessed to be part of such a great community where everyone makes me feel so welcome. The BEST feeling EVER to be back in the world of triathlon. I will smile a big smile all day for sure.

21.29

Absolutely blown away. So much so, I nearly fell out of my chair. So proud of my team. We came second today in the triathlon. All I wanted was to get round the course in about an hour or so. I was so well supported by other runners on the route. Volunteers, marshalling, spectators and even cars hooting as they passed! Paul and Judith caught up with me after their events and supported me all the way. How chuffed I feel to know I finished in 51.54 minutes. It really goes to show that teamwork helps you achieve things you didn't think possible.

August 8th

Today I feel a sense of panic. I keep getting palpitations. Today was my last day of being able-bodied and being able to walk. I had my last run. A most beautiful run too with my brown friend. I don't know why I'm panicking or feeling this way. I can't change the events that happened. I wouldn't want to either. I am really happy with my new life, I've had a amazing year. I think it's the brain's way of dealing with things subconsciously. My life is good but when a big trauma happens there are many stages you go through on your journey afterwards. This is just part of the journey. I will embrace it like everything else that has happened. The first year is a milestone and it's almost here.

18.41

Well, we've arrived near Beccles ready for the parachute jump tomorrow at noon! I'm feeling much more relaxed and happy. It's my wedding anniversary today, too. Quite ironic to be carried over the threshold of our caravan. It's a case of necessity now though, not just a romantic gesture. Vic has metaphorically carried the whole family in many ways since our anniversary last year. He has managed to hold down a full-time physical job and care for our four children whilst I was in hospital. He bought school uniforms and shoes when they started the autumn term last year. He went grocery shopping, took the kids  to all their clubs, cooked, cleaned, washed and hoovered. He kept our family together and supported me throughout. Since leaving hospital he has been devoted to caring for me and all my new needs. All marriages have struggles and difficulties. We have faced our biggest struggle.

It didn't break us, it made us stronger than ever. I'm so fortunate to have such an amazing man in my life. I don't mention Vic often on here but it seems appropriate today. I don't know where I'd be without him.

Vic, my husband is a very private man and throughout this whole journey I have hardly mentioned him on my Facebook posts. That is the way he likes it, though. He isn't one of these people who needs to broadcast to the world what he has done or how he feels. It is very obvious, though, that my accident would affect him and indeed it did. He remembers that day as he was walking out to his car, two policemen walked up to him to tell him of my accident. He thought they had come to tell him I was dead. He sobbed at my side when we were told that I would never walk again. Yet despite all the emotions and loss he was experiencing, he never crumpled but remained so strong and supportive for me and our children. It has brought us so close, yet some relationships struggle and break as a result of a life-changing experience.

I would say we were struggling with our relationship more before the accident. Life was hectic with children and work and university and all my running, and we seldom found time for each other. My accident made us both sit up and take stock of what we had together and so nearly lost. We cherish each other now and we find time together just to share a few moments for a chat or a hug. We laugh at the situations we find ourselves in. One of the best laughs we had was in the early days. Vic helped me out of the bath and as he lifted Bert and Ernie out he would always tap them on the edge of the bath to shake the drips off. He is very particular about mess, so he would not want them dripping on the foor. He would treat them as objects, not part of me. Then he would pull me by them in my shower chair back to the bedroom really fast. I guess you maybe had to be there, but it just always used to make us really laugh because it was just such an odd situation to find yourself in.

Vic says never in a million years did he expect to be pushing me in a wheelchair! He always imagined he would be the one who would deteriorate physically with the toils of his job, old age and that I would always be the fit, healthy one. Often when he sees me wheel up my ramp that he built outside the front door, he says I look so little and vulnerable and it melts his heart. We have really found each other through the tough times over the past year. We are a team and together we are so strong. Together we know that having been through this we can conquer anything. We will be together until the very end. 'Til death us do part!

August 9th

I think everyone would agree that this is a far better selfie than the one I posted last year. I don't think I realised the impact my hospital picture would have on everyone. I guess there is never going to be an easy way to tell anyone you aren't going to walk again. Today I echo the words I posted a year ago: 'Don't be sad or upset, I'm going to race you all in a pink racing chair.' I have already been racing, albeit not in a pink chair. Today is also a day to be happy and celebrate the amazing year I have had and how far I've come. It's not a day to be sad about my accident! To make the first year of my injury complete I am jumping out of a plane in a couple of hours. Life is meant to be lived, so live it to the full.

14.39

I'm a puky paraplegic parachutist!!

I didn't want the day of my first-year anniversary to be spent thinking back to the fated day and perhaps feeling a bit low and flat, especially after the fantastic year I had just had. No better distraction therefore than to jump out of a plane two and a half miles up in the sky falling at 120mph. Sitting on the edge of the plane with the earth laid out below me like a patchwork quilt was the best thing ever. I was literally on top of the world. Up here no one needed their legs, you flew. Free-falling was exhilerating. Such an adrenaline rush. Bitter cold wind whistling past you, deafening you. I was screaming but the screeching of the wind drowned out any sound I was making. Suddenly the noise just stopped as the chute opened and I felt myself being yanked back up in the sky. The instructor informed me that we were now safe. It was so peaceful just drifting down to earth. We had run through the procedure of how I was going to land because of the fact I was paralysed. I had to pull my legs up to my chest. Earlier on I had managed to do this as we were floating down, but as the jump progressed the instructor had to speed things up a bit as other jumpers were catching us. It got a bit scary here as the chute started to spin and I started to feel pretty sick. All the adrenaline had also turned me to jelly. At this point I realised that I could no longer lift my legs; the instructor urged me to keep trying. As we came in to land I just about managed to lift my right leg but my left one was dangling, which meant it could get broken as I landed. The instructor called to his colleagues on the ground to catch me. He shouted for them to run and one of them fell over. Just as we landed the other colleague managed to grab hold of my left leg and lift it up out of the way. I felt pretty sick and very wobbly and it took me a fair few hours to recover but it was an experience of a lifetime. I'm so proud that I did it. As far as I am concerned I finished off the year that marked the anniversary of my crash in the best way possible.

I think my year just shows that no matter who you are, you never know what is going to happen to you, but you can control how it affects you. Nothing has to be a big tragedy. You can turn it around into something positive. Life is what you want it to be no matter what it throws at you. Your destiny is your own and the sky has no limits.

Epilogue
August 9th 2016

Although the last diary entry in my book was in August, exactly a year ago today was the day that I came out of hospital. It was the day I really started my new life in a wheelchair. Who would have thought that so much could happen to one person in the space of a year. For starters I never thought I would be writing the finishing pages to a book. The day I lost control of my bike on Bury Hill, the door to my old life closed. People told me that when one door shuts, another opens. Well, not only did one open but loads of new doors opened with so many opportunities and adventures lying within.

I have laughed harder and cried harder this year than ever before. I also don't think I have ever worked as hard to achieve things in my life as I have over this past year. It has helped me to find a really deep inner determination not to be beaten but to bounce up and fight back stronger than ever. I think it has brought out the best in me and made me a more tolerant person. It has helped me to learn to be patient. It has taught me more than ever to be grateful for all that I have. I think it has helped me to try and accept people for who they are and to try and see the good in everyone. It has also made me realise how everyone going through life is struggling with their own battles. It has also helped my relationships with those I love grow stronger.

I have made friends and lost friends, but the friends I have lost can't have been that great or they would still be here and the friends that I have made have proved to be some of the best I could ever hope for. It has also taught me about how much I am loved and how special I truly am.

We have no idea what is going to happen in our lives; the only thing we can be sure of is that one day we will die. We also have no idea when that is going to be, so we need to live our life the best we can day by day. To me it's not about how much money I can make or how big my house is or the car I drive. It's not about how many holidays I go on or living the high life. To me this means making as big a difference as I can to the lives of those around me and maybe bring them some sort of comfort if they are struggling in life, too. I would like to be able to help others believe and be happy in themselves and be happy with what life gives them. To always believe that there is hope however hard things are and to never be afraid to ask for help. To not always be yearning for things that are bigger and better but to be able to appreciate the simple pleasures we can obtain from the small things around us. If my book helps just one person smile if they are struggling with life or to appreciate something they may have lost sight of, then the hours I have spent writing this book will be worth it.

Amanda Newton was born on the 2nd February 1971 and grew up in Chichester. She attended St Philip Howard RC secondary school and left with ten O levels and two A Levels.

She found her vocation in life when she met her husband to be Victor Worne, with whom she went on to have four children. They now live together in Yapton, West Sussex.

Amanda's children are her world and she devoted all her time to them. Whilst the children were growing up, Amanda had a number of part-time jobs that fitted in with her family. She also trained guide dogs for the blind and loved raising money for them through her running.

When Amanda's youngest son Joseph started school Amanda went back to university in Chichester and studied for a degree in Theology and Religion. She intended on using her degree to pursue her dream job, which was to work for the Guide Dogs for the Blind. Amanda had just finished her degree and had been offered an interview just weeks before her accident.

Since her accident in 2015, Amanda has been given a local hero award for being 'An Inspiration to Others'. She was chosen to be an Ambassador for a national campaign called 'Together We Will', which was set up to help raise awareness and encourage people with disabilities to become active. She promoted this campaign alongside the actor Will Mellor who had a sister with disabilities.

She has been a guest speaker at several events including The Regional Trauma conference at the American Express Community Stadium in Brighton and for the Scuba Trust charity at The Royal Geographical Society in London. She also works for Saltwater Creations giving workshops to schools, encouraging children to believe in themselves, offering help and ways to overcome challenges they may face and living life to the full.

Amanda continues to live in Yapton in her house that has just recently been transformed by the BBC television programme *DIY SOS*. She hopes that this book may just be the first of maybe a few as she still has many dreams she would like to pursue. She hopes to complete the London Marathon in 2018 and climb Mount Kilimanjaro in September 2017, perhaps using it as the title for her next book.

Amanda still posts almost every day on Facebook and you can follow her posts at www.facebook.com/amanda.newton.334.

She can also be contacted by email at Amanda.worne@hotmail.co.uk